THE
DECLINE AND FALL
OF THE
ROMANTIC IDEAL

THE
DECLINE AND FALL
OF THE
ROMANTIC IDEAL

BY

F. L. LUCAS

*Fellow of King's College
Cambridge*

CAMBRIDGE
AT THE UNIVERSITY PRESS
1963

PUBLISHED BY
THE SYNDICS OF THE CAMBRIDGE UNIVERSITY PRESS

Bentley House, 200 Euston Road, London, N.W. 1
American Branch: 32 East 57th Street, New York 22, N.Y.
West African Office: P.O. Box 33, Ibadan, Nigeria

First Edition	1936
Reprinted	1937
Second Edition	1948
Reprinted	1954
First Paperback Edition	1963

First printed in Great Britain at the University Press, Cambridge
Reprinted by offset-litho in the United States of America

To
a romantic
who has not declined nor fallen

GORDON BOTTOMLEY

CONTENTS

NOTE

An abridged version of chapters i–iii was delivered before the University College of North Wales at Bangor, as the three Ballard Mathews Lectures for 1935; and (in still shorter form) before the Royal Institution, in December of that year. Chapter v is a reprint of the Warton Lecture for 1933 to the British Academy, by whose permission it is republished here. I should like to express my gratitude to all three bodies for a kindness and hospitality that turned the lecturer's task into a pleasure.

I have added an Epilogue for reviewers and others who may find the book too long.

F. L. L.

August 1936

Nearly thirty years have passed since this book was written under the shadow of coming war. The War came; and provided a grimmer example than ever of the destructiveness of a Romanticism gone rotten. For Hitler, though he might pride himself on ruthless realism, remained, still more, a perverted romantic, who hated reason, boasted of marching to his goal like a somnambulist, and intoxicated both himself and his countrymen with megalomaniac dreams. And so, though far smaller than that other romantic, Napoleon, he proved even costlier. On the other hand I should like to make it clear from the outset that this book is *not* an indiscriminate attack on all Romanticism. Both life and literature have, I believe, reached their best with those that kept a steady, yet flexible, balance between Romanticism, Realism, and Classicism, all three. For it seems perilous to become either *too* imaginative, or *too* cynical, or *too* dominated even by good sense and great traditions. I have here tried to discuss both the triumphs and the dangers of Romanticism; the triumphs remain; but the dangers also.

Lilies that fester smell far worse than weeds.

F.L.L.

March 1963

CHAPTER I

LA PRINCESSE LOINTAINE; OR THE NATURE OF ROMANTICISM

THERE are two stanzas of Heine that all the world has heard:

> Ein Fichtenbaum steht einsam
> Im Norden auf kahler Höh.
> Ihn schläfert; mit weiszer Decke
> Umhüllen ihn Eis und Schnee.

> Er träumt von einer Palme,
> Die, fern im Morgenland,
> Einsam und schweigend trauert
> Auf brennender Felsenwand.

> On a bare northern hillside
>   A lonely fir-tree grows,
> Nodding in its white mantle
>   Of ice and driven snows.

> And of a palm its dream is
>   That sorrows, mute, alone,
> In some far land of morning
>   On hills of burning stone.

Many modern critics would say this was a bad poem. A Nazi would say it was a very bad poem. It was written by a Jew; and all poems by Jews are execrable. This criterion has at least the merit of simplicity. Others would say: "It is a Romantic poem; and all Romantic poems are worthless". Or, to turn back to an older judge, more serious though hardly less severe, suppose we called up, like the ghost of another Samuel at Endor, the ghost of Samuel Johnson? The ghost would, I think, have snorted. "What pleasure or instruction are we to derive

from an enormous and disgusting hyperbole that tells
us how one vegetable sighs for another vegetable; which,
even if vegetables could hear or see, it could never have
seen nor heard of; nor coveted, if it had. If the moral
be the vanity of human wishes, that moral can but too
easily be pointed on our own doorsteps, without trans-
porting us on the wings of absurdity to the snows of
Norway or the sands of Palmyra. Better even that poem
of Erasmus Darwin on *The Loves of the Plants*, which was
produced five years after my death in the Lichfield of
my birth; and describes, to those who can read it,

> What Beaux and Beauties crowd the gaudy groves
> And woo and win their vegetable Loves.
>
> Sweet blooms Genista in the myrtle shade
> And *ten* fond brothers woo the haughty maid...
> Woo'd with long care, Curcuma[1] cold and shy
> Meets her fond husband with averted eye:
> Four beardless youths the obdurate beauty move
> With soft attentions of Platonic love...
> The freckled Iris owns a fiercer flame,
> And *three* unjealous husbands wed the dame;
> Cupressus dark disdains his dusky bride,
> *One* dome contains them, but *two* beds divide.

Here there is science at least, if there be but little sense."

And yet, despite the principles of Dr Johnson, Heine's
fir and palm have found a lasting place among his
laurels; they remain, despite the bonfires of Dr Goebbels,
equally evergreen; while Dr Darwin's plants, typical
products of the autumn of Classicism, droop ludicrously
bedraggled in their polished hothouse. Good or bad,
I have quoted Heine's lyric because it seems to me not
only an essentially Romantic poem, but also a poem
about the essence of Romance.

[1] The Turmeric.

For it is a dream-poem. Its melody soothes asleep the Argus-eyes of common sense; unless, like Johnson, we rigidly maintain the vigilance of some Classic dragon, guarding the sacred fruit of Reason; of some Roman sentry sternly wakeful at the gates of Fact. And, again, it is a poem about a dream; about the bitter-sweetness of all passionate yearning for things so remote that only in dream can they be ours. It utters the dumb cry of all hands stretched out for that fairy gold on which the rainbow stands—symbol, for the Bible, of God's eternal promise; but for the Romantic, of Man's eternal unfulfilment. Fantastic as Heine's poem seems, it yet embodies impulses real enough to have played no humble part in bringing Alaric to the gates of Rome, the Crusaders to Antioch and Ascalon, Columbus to Hispaniola.

But what remains to-day the worth of this Romanticism, on which the modern wise gaze so coldly askance; though the modern multitude scrambles after its magic pipings as feverishly as ever, through picture-palace and circulating library? This is the question on which I have rashly set out to try to say something new—shall we still allow fir-trees to dream? Or does that simply send us to sleep? Do we belong too much, for better or worse, to an age not of fir-trees but of steel girders? Or can even girders learn to dream?—even ferro-concrete be transmuted to the fabric of fantasy?

"The worst of romances is", said Oscar Wilde, "that they leave one so unromantic." In the same way the reader who gnaws his way through the 11,396 books on Romanticism, begins to feel cured of Romance for life. And that, I think (though so many now think otherwise), is a pity. Why, then, try to write still more about it? Why add to the dustheap? "There is no new thing under the sun"—that dismal judgement of Solomon must indeed haunt us as we peer into the vast bibliographies of such a subject. And it will haunt our children still worse, our grandchildren worse still; unless libraries are abolished by international agreement or— as seems more likely—by international disagreement.

And yet it is foolish to be afraid of the thin elbowings of the dead. When Solomon cried that there was no new thing, he was forgetting himself. *He* was new. Like everyone else before or since, he was unlike everyone else before or since. Facts are facts, the past is past—we cannot change them. Yet in another sense we are perpetually changing them. What we call "the World" is a compound of the unknown It and our novel and unique selves. In the Sciences, men's impressions are so similar that they can be treated as identical. There knowledge accumulates; progress becomes possible. But in the Arts, and even in the Art of Criticism, we must still walk our own ways to the end. Tradition helps; but, when all is said, we can sing, we can taste, with no tongues but our own. Each new generation, each new life creates a new universe.

And so I am daring to add yet another to those 11,396 discussions of Romanticism. But I shall deal only briefly with older theories; and I shall not feel all is lost, if my readers harden their heads against the new theory that I offer now.

"For God's sake disagree with me," cried Cicero's young friend to the obsequious country-cousin at lunch with him, "so that there can be two of us." So now, if the reader does not agree with me about Romanticism, still he may find how to agree better with himself. For no one discovers what he really thinks, till he has crossed thoughts with others. So much criticism becomes charlatanism only because the critic wants to say, not his word, but the last word. The only way to be scientific about Art is to recognize that we cannot yet be scientific about Art. We know too little psychology. Even of Science Montesquieu has well said that "observations are its facts, theories its fairy-tales". If this theory proves only one more fairy-tale, I hope some of its examples and illustrations may yet be interesting in and for themselves.

"There may be a good deal to be said for Romanticism in life, there is no place for it in letters"—so writes one modern critic, with that trenchant decisiveness not uncommon in men of the pen; at least on paper. "There is no place in letters", that is, for Coleridge or Scott, Keats or Emily Brontë, Hugo or Heine? But, it will be said, this is mad. What possible purpose can be served by such oracular dogmatism? The purpose of amassing a reputation. Men are easily brow-beaten about Art. Accordingly our criticism flourishes on a brazen standard. And yet how comes such a statement to be made in the country of Coleridge and Keats? Because it had already been made in the country of Victor Hugo and Alfred de Musset. But is it any saner to say it in France? Hardly. But more intelligible. For behind it rankle the long embitterments of French politics.

"Le Romantisme, c'est la Révolution"—"le Romantisme, c'est Rousseau." Rousseau's work, we are told, "exhale une odeur de cadavre". From him came "cette corruption intégrale des hautes parties de la nature

humaine"—"la pourriture *romantique* de l'intelligence".[1]
Those who have heard the tone with which this last
endearment, "pourriture", can be bandied between
two Parisian taxi-drivers in the throes of collision, will
feel that the very last word has been said.

Romanticism is, in fact, to be identified with Liberalism. "Chateaubriand", says M. Charles Maurras, "was
all his life a liberal or—what comes to the same thing—
an anarchist." This is at least a new view of Chateaubriand, of liberalism, and of anarchy. The wonder does
not diminish as we ask ourselves what were the "anarchist" tendencies in Alfred de Vigny; or in Scott, that
devoted Tory who so religiously treasured (till unfortunately he sat down on it) the very wineglass from which
Majesty had drunk; or try to picture Newman or
Christina Rossetti waving red flags, Disraeli or Walter
Pater leading the legions of Limehouse to storm St
Stephen's. No doubt rebellion in art and rebellion in
politics often have gone hand in hand; but far from
always. Life is less simple. A principle of compensation
may come into play; it would be easy to name modern
journals which uphold both the right in politics and the
left in literature. "See," they seem to say, "we are not
afraid of innovation—in the right place." Actually, the
French Revolution found its spiritual home largely in
the republics of classic Greece and Rome, among the
men of Plutarch. Its painter, David, loathed the mediaeval. The Classicism of the Empire speaks for itself.
Even after Waterloo it was the Romantic leaders who
were legitimist and Catholic. Similarly, German Roman-

---

[1] See Maurice Souriau's interesting *Hist. du Romantisme en France*,
pp. xxvii–xxxvi.

ticism brought miraculous draughts of converts to the nets of Rome. Even in modern Germany the Nazi movement shows a strong "Romantic" tinge with its homesick hankerings to revert to the noble pagan, to Nature and the soil, to "thinking with the blood"—all the queer nostrums it shares with that modern Rousseau, D. H. Lawrence. So that to blame Romanticism for the sins of the Revolution seems a little like proclaiming, because Marx admired Shakespeare and Moscow performs him, that the Prince of Denmark was a disguised Bolshevik and King Lear the ancestor of Lenin.

Such fantasies are possible, partly because human beings will believe anything in the heat of controversy; but partly also because critics still tend to ignore other literatures than their own. English critics to-day still make glib generalizations about "poetry", which they would see to be absurd had they thought for two minutes about the poetry of other countries. Similarly, French critics can treat "the Romantics" in general as public poisoners, because in France, with French logic and French fire, men and women did try far more to live as well as write "Romantically"; often with disastrous results that have had few counterparts on our colder side of the Channel. It is enough to set Tennyson with his almost Philistine healthiness, his growls about "poisonous honey brought from France", beside Alfred de Musset; or Browning beside Victor Hugo; or George Eliot beside George Sand; or Meredith beside Flaubert. Think, again, of the Young England movement beside *les Jeune-France*—of all our muscular Christians, muscular deists, muscular agnostics, whose robustness Taine admired as might some explorer coming suddenly in a jungle-clearing upon a herd of moon-lit elephants. But in France, Flaubert and the Goncourts looked askance at Taine with his outlandish notions of healthiness in art: they were half convinced that to be an artist one must be sick, as whales to produce ambergris.[1] Naturally two countries so different bred very different forms of Romanticism.

Thus the French intelligence, after its wont, reasoned out far clearer theories of the Romantic; French consistency carried them to wilder extremes in practice; and, in the reaction that naturally followed, the French intelligence has evolved still more theories of the universal disastrousness of Romanticism. These are, I think, partly true of Romanticism in France; but they are very imperfectly true of Romanticism in general. In England they often fail to apply at all.

There is the further trouble that the word "Romanticism" has turned from a historical label into a war-cry. No one knows quite what it does mean. And it is clear that "Classicism" has suffered the same fate, when modern poets who cultivate, however successfully, the Romantic incoherence of an opium dream, the rhythms of the music-hall, and the vocabulary of the slum—all the things that would have jarred to frenzy Pope, Johnson, or Boileau—proudly profess and call themselves "Classical".

[1] Cf. Michelet's remark when Flaubert is suffering from boils—"Qu'il ne se soigne pas, il n'aurait plus son talent". The Goncourts had the same crotchet about themselves. Cf. too J. Renard, *Journal*, 1 August 1898: "L'esprit vit aux dépens du corps; si tu te portes bien, tu penseras mal." It would surely be truer to say: "You will have fewer fantasies." It is simply a question of whether one prefers auto-intoxicated dreaming or the clear-headedness of health.

What in fact is "Romanticism"? What, historically, has it been? What can or should it be?

What is it? It will be well to begin with a few of the answers of past critics; together with antidotes in the style of Diogenes. The story is well known. Plato had defined man as "a featherless biped"; Diogenes promptly paraded the streets of Athens displaying a plucked fowl to the world as "Plato's man". Diogenes may not have been a very good philosopher; he is very good indeed for philosophers.

"Romanticism", said Goethe, "is disease; Classicism is health." And again—"the point is for a work to be thoroughly good and then it is sure to be Classical". So the author of *Werther* cuts the knot, leaving us only loose ends. For, after all, is *The Ancient Mariner* really "diseased"? Is *Faust* not "Romantic"?

Stendhal cuts the knot as trenchantly; but in a different direction. For him Romanticism is, at any time, the art of the day; Classicism, the art of the day before. In fact, all good art is first Romantic, then becomes Classical. And yet, does anyone, even after a century, think of *The Ancient Mariner* as Classical? Or *The Lady of Shalott*? We may call them "classics", meaning "established masterpieces". But that is another story. To use "Romantic" as a mere synonym for "up-to-date" does not leave us wiser; it merely leaves the language poorer.

The Dictionary of the French Academy in 1835 and some later critics have preferred to treat "Romanticism" as a matter simply of technique—a mere kicking against the pricks of Classicism, as governed by the Rules, say, of Boileau. But this seems too negative. Zola, or many a modern writer who detests Romanticism, would have been no less detested by Boileau. Romanticism cannot be made merely the opposite of Classicism; because Classicism has, I think, more opposites than one.

Victor Hugo in his famous preface to *Cromwell* preferred to associate Romanticism above all with "the grotesque". Christianity, he argues, with its sense of sin brought melancholy into the world (surely one of the strangest assertions ever made). Man now realized the paradox of his imperfect nature—

> Magnificent out of the dust we came,
> And abject from the spheres.[1]

With this melancholy grew up the sense of "the grotesque"—whether horrible, or ludicrous, or both (like Hugo's own Hunchback); and hence arose that habit of mingling the grotesque with the tragic or sublime, which Classicism forbids, but life confirms. Thus, after signing Charles I's death-warrant, Cromwell and another of the regicides are said to have bespattered each other's faces with the ink. Romanticism is therefore really Truthfulness (*la vérité*).

Yet what, we may ask, is "grotesque" in Wordsworth's *Highland Maid* or in Keats's *La Belle Dame sans Merci*, in Musset's *Nuits* or Yeats's *Inisfree*?

Later Hugo was content to define Romanticism more vaguely, as "liberalism in literature"; or merely as a "mot de guerre".

For Heine, Romanticism was "the reawakening of the Middle Ages...a passion-flower blooming from the blood of Christ"; Sismondi, too, has defined it by its themes, as a mixture of love, religion and chivalry. And

[1] William Watson.

yet there is nothing mediaeval in *Werther* or *Wuthering Heights*;[1] little religion in Byron or Morris; little love in *Kubla Khan*. It remains, I think, as hard to define Romanticism by its subjects or its sympathies, as by its style and technique.

Others have approached Romanticism by its emotional temper. To Brunetière, in so far as it was more than a mere reaction from Classicism, it seemed a blind wave of literary egotism. It must be admitted that many Romantics were extravagantly self-centred. Lord Chesterfield would have considered that Chateaubriand or Byron, as writers, had no manners. But is *The Ancient Mariner*, that invaluable example, egotistic?—is it not, on the contrary, a sermon against egotism? What of Scott? What of Keats, with his opposite theory that the true poet is, like Shakespeare, a selfless sympathy inhabiting the shoes and the very skins of others; entering the heart now of Imogen, now of a sparrow, now of Iago, now of a billiard-ball?

"Emotion against Reason"—so runs another of the most time-worn formulas for the Romantic Revolt. George Sand has written: "Everything excessive is poetic". And Léon Daudet, with his usual restraint, has described Romanticism in general as "une espèce de codification du dérèglement... une béatification de l'impulsivité". Yet the heroine of *The Heart of Midlothian* is a stoic who refuses to perjure herself even to save a sister's life; and Scott's own Journal remains a monument of sanity and honesty, courage and self-control. The whole life of Christina Rossetti was a tragedy of morbid

[1] Heine's view is admirably dealt with and answered in Professor Grierson's Leslie Stephen lecture for 1923—*Classical and Romantic*.

self-repression. Nor was eighteenth-century Classicism so unemotional: think of Swift dying "like a poisoned rat in its hole"; of Voltaire, of whom it has been well said that we might as well call white-hot iron "cold", because it is not red. He could not even understand, he cried, how people *could* be cold. He found too frigid the acting of Mlle Dumesnil. "Il faudrait avoir le diable au corps", she complained, "pour arriver au ton que vous me voulez faire prendre." "Eh vraiment, oui, c'est le diable au corps qu'il faut avoir *pour exceller dans tous les arts*." Think, too, of Johnson, so much more emotional than most of us, that in boyhood *Hamlet* made him afraid to go to bed and even in manhood he could not face the end of *Lear*. And what of the passion of the "Classical" *Phèdre*, the horrors of the "Classical" *Oedipus*?

Others have concentrated on the general atmosphere of Romantic works. For Pater Romanticism was the addition of "strangeness" to beauty; yet it has often aimed not at beauty at all, but quite other things, such as the terrible or the grotesque. For Watts-Dunton it was "the Renascence of Wonder", after "the periwig poetry" of the eighteenth century; for others it is "mystery" or "aspiration". Romantic literature, they might say, is Wonderland; whereas Classic literature is a Looking-glass world, coldly reflecting reality in its gilded Queen Anne frame. And yet there is surely little "mystery", ever, in Byron or Swinburne, in Burns or Musset; often, there is little "aspiration".

Professor Abercrombie has transferred the conflict to a fresh front. For him Romanticism is the opposite, not of Classicism, but of Realism. Shakespeare he finds as "Classical" as Sophocles, except in the early phase of

Richard II and *Romeo and Juliet*. By "Realism", however, Professor Abercrombie means, not the literary creed of a Zola, but "the habit of mind" of a Bentham. "Romanticism is a withdrawal from outer experience to concentrate on inner experience"—as in Blake, or Shelley, or "cubist painting".

There is far more truth, I think, in this view; but it seems to me both to exaggerate and to omit. Hugo, it will be recalled, justified Romanticism as, on the contrary, a return to reality; because real life perpetually mingles hornpipes and funerals to compose its ironic "Satires of Circumstance". It was Classicism that cried out against the crudity of even naming so low an animal as a dog or so vulgar an object as Desdemona's handkerchief. "Enlevez-moi ces magots!" exclaimed Louis XIV, on being shown some realistic Dutch pictures. Similarly Schiller, adapting in Classic mood the Romantic pages of *Macbeth*, felt it necessary to replace the raw conversation of the Porter by a morning hymn about sky-larks.

What, again, could be more realistic than the low life in Scott's romances, or the carpets rising along the gusty floor in *The Eve of St Agnes*? Morris thought nothing of a mediaevalist who could not draw offhand a knight in armour with his feet on the hob, toasting a herring on his sword-point; and in his work who has not seen and felt, so vivid are they, the grey ears of Lancelot's horse twitching on the dusty downs by Glastonbury, the beads of melted snow-water on the steel shoes of Sir Galahad, the mud and rain and cold and hopelessness of that sodden Haystack in the Floods? Similarly with the minute realism of Pre-Raphaelite painting. It was, in fact, this love of the Romantics for realistic *décor* and setting,

furniture and local colour, that provided one source of
Naturalism in the later novel. They grasped the importance of environment, the power of material adjuncts
over the soul. The rustics of Scott and Sand look forward
to the rustics of Hardy and Maupassant; the Paris of
Hugo to the Paris of Balzac. So far is there from being an
impassable gulf between Romance and Realism that
Charlotte's homely bread-and-butter has stuck for ever
to the Romantic sleeve of Werther; and Wordsworth,
having launched his Highland Boy first of all, only too
realistically, in

> A Household Tub, like one of those,
> Which women use to wash their clothes,

was yet ready to trans-ship him, at Coleridge's persuasion, to a Romantic turtle-shell—

> A shell of ample size, and light
> As the pearly car of Amphitrite,
> That sportive dolphins drew.

The Romantic is in fact ready to swallow the most
realistic herring, provided it is on the point of a sword—
or merely to annoy the Classicist who thinks it "low".
"All very well," said Lockhart of Mr Pickwick, "but
damned low"; Dickens, like Browning, shows how easy
it is to alternate between Realism and Romance. It was
Classicism that found itself accused at the Romantic
Revival of never "having its eye on the object". Similarly with a writer like Flaubert it is hard to say whether
he is more romantic or realistic. His *Salammbô* was
archaeologically minute to the point of pedantry. Yet
he not only created Emma Bovary; he was himself Emma
Bovary, a romantic dreamer. He enjoyed the paradoxes

of his own double nature. He loved to contemplate the stars in puddles. The contrasts of the Orient fascinated him—its perfumes and its vermin, the silver bracelet on the ulcered arm, the plague-stricken corpses among the golden oranges of Jaffa. "Tu me dis que les punaises de Ruchiouk-Hânem" (a famous Egyptian courtesan) "te la dégradent; c'est là, moi, ce qui m'enchantait. Leur odeur nauséabonde se mêlait au parfum de sa peau ruisselante de santal." It is quite understandable. The Romantic pursues violent feelings; and, like an Elizabethan dramatist, he may find them in the crudities of reality as well as in the fantasies of dream. Indeed, dreams themselves can be at times only too realistic.

In short, the learned are no nearer agreement now than when Alfred de Musset made comedy of the whole controversy in the first of those *Lettres de Dupuis et Cotonet* which are too little known in England. Dupuis and Cotonet, two good provincials of La-Ferté-sous-Jouarre and surely next-of-kin to Flaubert's Bouvard and Pécuchet, write to the *Revue des Deux Mondes* the sad story of their quest—what *is* Romanticism? At first they thought it meant breaking the Unities; then, after Hugo's *Cromwell*, that it was the wedding of sublime and grotesque; then that it meant imitating foreigners and importing gnomes, ghouls, vampires, ogres and mandrakes from Germany, melancholia from England, tempestuous passions from Andalusia and Castile; then that it meant playing ducks and drakes with the rules of French prosody; then that it was "le genre historique"— novels about François I and the like; then that it was "le genre intime"—whatever that might mean; then that it was a system of political economy; then that it meant going about unshaven in a flamboyant waistcoat. In vain they consulted làwyers' clerks and local magistrates; these only added to their confusion. Until at last Cotonet discovered the whole simple truth; Romanticism consists in stringing round the neck of every noun at least half a dozen epithets. In this year 1936 Dupuis and Cotonet celebrate their centenary; but their old age remains as green as their ingenuous youth.[1]

Clearly the first thing is to dig back to the roots. What is the origin of these two quarrelsome words, "Classic" and "Romantic"? The point has often been discussed but it cannot be neglected; and there are certain details that have not, I think, been fully brought out.

As the Roman Empire was flooded by the barbarians, beside official Latin—*lingua Latina*—there grew up a barbarized vernacular called, by the eighth century, "*lingua Romanica*". From its adverb *Romanice* (*loqui* or *scribere*) comes the noun "Romance"; applied first to

[1] No doubt, just as MM. Maurras and Daudet have explained Romanticism by politics, other Dupuis and Cotonets of the future will arise to explain it, Marxianly, by economics. They will not be deterred by the reflection that the great Romantics included all sorts and conditions of men—Rousseau and Chateaubriand, Vigny and Stendhal, Walpole and Chatterton, Burns and Byron, Keats and Shelley, Swinburne and Meredith. But I doubt if we can say much more than that the passing of power from upper to middle class and the spread of education did certainly affect the public for which writers wrote, and thereby what they wrote. Aristocracies tend more to sacrifice feeling to *les bienséances*, the *bourgeoisie* to think more of morals but less of manners, more of the heart and less of "that repose Which marks the caste of Vere de Vere". This doubtless helped the emotionalism of nineteenth-century literature to break down the rigid traditions of the eighteenth; just as the vast further extension of the reading public may account for some of the literary vulgarity of the twentieth. And of course the emotional effect of the French Revolution is a commonplace. But Romanticism remains, I think, essentially a problem, not of politics or economics, but of psychology.

old French (*romanz*), then to Provençal (*roumanço*) and Spanish (*romance*); later still to the other Latin tongues. Again, from meaning the French vernacular the word came to denote also the kind of literature composed in that vernacular—that is, fictitious stories in verse or, later, prose. In the seventeenth century appears a new development. From its fictitious nature "romance" comes, like "fable", to mean any fantastic statement. And "romantic" now signifies either "false as a fairy-tale", or "strange and dream-like as a fairy-tale".[1] It is easy to find similar developments in words like "tragic", "comic", "dramatic", "melodramatic", "dithyrambic", "quixotic". "These things", writes Pepys, "are almost romantique, and yet true"; and his brother-diarist, Evelyn: "There is also, on the side of this horrid alp, a very romantic seat". The first recorded appearances of this whole family of usages in the *Oxford Dictionary* group themselves with surprising neatness round the middle of the seventeenth century—"a romance", as a lying tale, 1638: "romance", as an adjective, 1653–4 ("Can there be a romancer story than ours?" writes Dorothy Osborne); "romancial", 1653; "romancical", 1656; "romancy", 1654; "romantic", meaning "fictitious", 1659; "romantical", 1678; "romanticly", 1681 ("romantickly or fabulously"); "romantically", 1687; "romancer", meaning "liar", 1663; "to romance", 1671. This sudden flowering of new

---

[1] The similar growth of "romanesque" in French is illustrated by the comments of "Madame", the Duchess of Orleans, on Villars in her letters to the Electress of Hanover (ed. E. Bodemann, 1891): "Alle des Marechal de Villars maniren seindt *romanesque*" (May 30, 1706); "V. fehlt nicht von verstandt undt hatt grosz courage, aber...ist recht *wie ein lebendiger roman*" (July 28, 1707).

and somewhat uncomplimentary terms was probably
helped by the popular romances of Mlle de Scudéry
and her kind on the one hand and, on the other, by
the growing reaction from things fantastic in favour of
"reason". In the eighteenth century the better sense,
"strange as a romance", gradually tends to prevail. The
word attaches itself to Gothic ruins, wild landscapes,
and other delightful mixtures of terror and sublimity,
such as banditti.

Its literary sense—as opposed, like "Gothic", to
"Classical"—appears in T. Warton (1781) and Hurd.[1]
But it was the Germans, with their love of abstract
discussion, who developed the contrast. Goethe claims
that he and Schiller first set this apple of discord rolling.
Schiller calls his *Jungfrau von Orleans* "eine romantische
Tragödie" (1802); A. W. von Schlegel uses the term in
his lectures (1801–4), followed by Madame de Staël in
her *De l'Allemagne* (1810). It can be appropriately
applied, argues Schlegel, to work of *mediaeval* inspiration
by contrast with what is "Classical", in the same way
as "Romance", the language evolved by the barbarian
invaders, is opposed to the classical Latin of the
Empire.

Such, then, is the word's pedigree. "Romance"
means first a certain language; then a certain type of
literature composed in that language; then the epithet
"romantic" is applied to the unreality associated with
that type of literature; or to the temperament associated

---

[1] I am indebted for these two references to Logan Pearsall Smith,
Four Words (S.P.E. Tract No. xvii). Warton speaks of Dante's "wonderful
compound of classical and romantic fancy" (*Hist. of Eng. Poetry* (1781),
iii, 241).

with that type of unreality; or to the literary forms associated with that type of temperament.

"Classical" is a gentleman of more ancient descent. In Latin *classis* (perhaps from the same root as "call") meant originally "a host", military as well as naval. Good King Tullius divided his citizens into five grades, according to the arms they could afford. The richest, providing the cavalry and the heavy-armed phalanx (*classis*), were called *classici*; the rest were *infra classem*. But *classicus* is not transferred metaphorically to writers until, seven centuries later, under the Empire, Aulus Gellius contrasts *classicus scriptor* with *proletarius*—"a first-class, standard writer" with "one of the rabble". At the Renaissance the fact that the "standard" writers of Greece and Rome were read *in class* at school seems to have helped by confusion to produce that other sense of "classic", as applied to any Greek or Roman writer, whether first-class or not. Thus "classical", meaning "standard", dates, in the *Oxford Dictionary*, from 1599 ("Classicall and Canonicall"); meaning "Greek or Latin", from 1607 ("classicall Authors"). Thence the epithet adapted itself to anything supposed to conform to the standards of classical antiquity.

Still, what a word meant once upon a time, though illuminating, is no proof of what it means now (though critics have too often forgotten this and argued, for example, in the teeth of common usage, that because *poiesis* in Greek means any "creative literature" in verse or prose alike, "poetry" in English need not be in metre). As we have seen, "Romanticism" is a perfect Proteus for eluding all our nets of definition. But it is not so much its logical definition, as its psychological basis that really matters: it is more informative to study an elephant in the flesh than to labour overlong at defining it.

The term "Romantic" has to-day two main usages; first, as applied in a historic sense to the movement which called itself "Romantic"; secondly, to describe other things which give us the same sort of feeling as, say, *La Belle Dame sans Merci* or *The Ancient Mariner* or *Atala* or Hugo's song of Gastibelza. This more general sense is, of course, really older and based originally on the romances of the seventeenth century. But they are now forgotten. It is the masterpieces of the Romantic Revival that have inevitably moulded our modern standards of what is "romantic". The French, indeed, have two words: "romantique" for the movement; "roman-esque" for the feeling.[1] But the essential question remains what, if any, are the common qualities of the mental states in which we are moved to make the noise— "How romantic!"

It is worth trying first what sort of examples the word spontaneously calls to memory. A little free association will help.

Lady of the Mere
Sole-sitting by the shores of old romance.

"Forlorn"—the very word is like a bell.

The foam
Of perilous seas, in faery lands forlorn.

Antres vast and deserts idle.

And airy tongues, that syllable men's names
On Sands and Shoars and desert Wildernesses.

[1] I have tried to preserve this not unserviceable distinction by using "Romantic" with a capital in speaking of the movement, as the equivalent of "romantique"; and "romantic" in the general sense, corresponding to "romanesque".

"On dirait des silences qui succèdent à des silences."[1]
"J'ai jeté mon anneau dans les forêts."[2] "The owl for all
his feathers was a-cold." "The sedge is withered from
the lake."

> La Belle Dame sans Merci
> Hath thee in thrall.

> A casement ope at night
> To let the warm Love in.

"Quel giorno più non vi leggemmo avante." "Où sont
les neiges d'antan?" "Sunt apud infernos tot milia
formosarum."[3] The ghost of Elsinore. "Or woman
wailing for her demon lover." Bürger's *Lenore*. *North-
anger Abbey*. *Wuthering Heights* (with the young Hareton
hanging a litter of puppies on a chair-back to pass a
happy afternoon).

> The worms they crept in, and the worms they crept out,
> And sported his eyes and his temples about.[4]

> Son cœur les bêtes l'ont mangé,
> Qu'en reste-t-il pour sa donzelle?
> Rien qu'un amas en vers changé,
> Rien qu'un paquet de vermicelle.[5]

> The day doth daw, the cock doth craw,
>   The channerin' worm doth chide.

> Hic tibi mortis erant metae, domus alta sub Ida,
> Lyrnesi domus alta, solo Laurente sepulchrum.[6]

"And Branwen looked towards Ireland, and towards
the Isle of the Mighty, to see if she could descry them.
'Alas,' said she, 'that ever I was born; two islands have

---

[1] Chateaubriand.
[2] Ducis (alluding to the Doge's wedding with the sea).
[3] Propertius.
[4] "Monk" Lewis, *Alonzo the Brave and the Fair Imogene*.
[5] Verhaeren.   [6] Virgil.

been destroyed because of me.' Then she gave a great groan and there broke her heart. And they made her a four-sided grave and buried her on the banks of the Alaw."[1]

ἀεὶ δ'ἀνὰ νύκτα καὶ ἠῶ
ἐξ ἁλὸς ἠνεμοέντος ἐπιβρέμει οὔασιν ἠχώ.[2]

"Es war ein König in Thule."[3]   "Les violons vibrant derrière les collines."[4]

Le vent qui vient à travers la montagne
Me rendra fou.[5]

"Is there anybody there?" said the Traveller,
Knocking on the moonlit door.[6]

Still eyes look coldly upon me,
Cold voices whisper and say:
"He is crazed with the spell of far Arabia,
They have stolen his wits away."[7]

A chain hangs down with golden fetters
From a green oak-tree, in a bay,
And on that chain a cat of letters
Walks round for ever, night and day;
Goes singing, as she rightward ambles;
Turns leftward, and a tale relates.
Strange things are there: the wood-sprite rambles;
The water-maid in branches waits;
And there, on paths unnoted, thickens
The slot of beasts to man unknown;
A cottage there on legs of chickens,
Unwindowed, doorless, stands alone.[8]

---

[1] *The Mabinogion.*   [2] Musaeus, *Hero and Leander.*
[3] Goethe.   [4] Baudelaire.   [5] Hugo.
[6] Walter de la Mare, *The Listeners* (it should be remembered—I have it on the poet's authority—that the Traveller is himself the ghost).
[7] Walter de la Mare.
[8] Pushkin (transl. O. Elton): an almost surrealistic passage.

Our only Gods shall be the Subterrane
Pictures of things mis-shapen, harsh, and crude,
The flattened Face outside the window-pane,
The little Squeak behind us in the wood.
Here, friend, are subtly drawn uncommon things;
Make such your Gods; they only understand.
Only a Headless Ape with slimy wings
Can whisk you round the Interesting Land.[1]

With an host of furious fancies
Whereof I am commander,
With a burning speare, and a horse of aire,
To the wildernesse I wander.
By a knight of ghostes and shadowes
I summon'd am to tourney
Ten leagues beyond the wide world's end.
Mee thinkes it is noe journey.[2]

The town of Brass in the *Arabian Nights*. The ruins of
Frankish Mistra, above the ancient Lacedaemon, which
inspired a scene in the Second Part of *Faust*.

Far in the town of Sarras
    Red-rose the gloamings fall,
For in her heart of wonder
    Flames the Sangreal.

The gleaming fosses ring her,
    Haut dreams her turrets are,
She riseth o'er the desert,
    Like the great Magian star.[3]

"The back-tolled bells of noisy Camelot."[4] "After
these years the flowers forget their blood."[4] The words
of the Earl of Derby (later Henry IV) above the dying
Sir William Ramsay: "Ah, it is a goodly sight to see
a Knight make his shrift in his helmet. God send me such

---

[1] Flecker (an example of Hugo's "grotesque").
[2] *Tom o' Bedlam*.   [3] Rachel Annand Taylor.
[4] Morris.

an ending!" Sir John Mandeville's "Watching of the Falcon". The Venus of Botticelli.

> C'est chose bien commune
> De soupirer pour une
> Blonde, chataîne, ou brune
>   Maîtresse,
>
> Lorsque brune, chataîne,
> Ou blonde, on l'a sans peine—
> Moi, j'aime la lointaine
>   Princesse.[1]

"It is an odd jealousy; but the poet finds himself not near enough to his object. The pine-tree, the river, the bank of flowers before him, does not seem to be nature. Nature is still elsewhere. This or this is but outskirt and far-off reflection and echo of the triumph that has passed by and is now at its glancing splendour and heyday, perchance in the neighbouring fields, or, if you stand in the field, then in the adjacent woods. The present object shall give you this sense of stillness that follows a pageant that has just gone by. What splendid distance, what recesses of ineffable pomp and loveliness in the sunset! But who can go where they are, or lay his hand or plant his foot thereon? Off they fall from the round world for ever and for ever."[2]

"Toutes les femmes qu'il a eues n'ont jamais été que les matelas d'une autre femme rêvée."[3]

Such are some of the spirits, fair or grotesque, called up for me by the word "Romance"—some of the things for which, we are told, "there is no place in literature". What are the qualities that recur? Remoteness, the sad delight of desolation, silence and the supernatural, winter and dreariness; vampirine love and stolen trysts,

---

[1] Rostand.   [2] Emerson.
[3] *Journal* of the Goncourts (a confession of Flaubert's); note again the combination of Realism with Romance in the phrasing.

the flowering of passion and the death of beauty; Radcliffe horrors and sadistic cruelty, disillusion, death, and madness; the Holy Grail and battles on the Border; the love of the impossible. Before looking for the essential common factor of this strange miscellany it will be as well to repeat the experiment with the terms "Classicism", "Classical". What do they in their turn call to mind?[1]

The Parthenon. The tomb-reliefs of the Ceramīcus. The grave Roman faces of the Ara Pacis. "The Dorian mood of flutes and soft recorders." The Regulus of Horace, going as calmly to death by torture at Carthage as to a week-end in the country—

> Tendens Venafranos in agros
> Aut Lacedaemonium Tarentum.

The epitaph of Simonides on the Spartans at Thermopylae. The Delphic "Μηδὲν ἄγαν". The epitaph of the Roman Claudia:

> This is the loveless tomb of one once lovely.
> Comely her speech was, graceful was her going.
> She kept house; spun her wool. 'Tis all. Farewell.

Horace's:

> Aequam memento rebus in arduis
> Servare mentem.

Denham's Thames:

> Though deep, yet clear: though gentle, yet not dull:
> Strong, without rage: without o'erflowing, full.

[1] This multiplication of examples may seem long: but the fatal weakness of critical discussions like that between Wordsworth and Coleridge on "Poetic Diction" is their failure to give examples enough; with the result that neither disputant really knows what he means.

The flower-like simplicity of André Chénier's—

> Elle a vécu, Myrto, la jeune Tarentine,
> Que son vaisseau portait aux bords de Camarine.

The death of Odysseus' last companions, lost at sea—
"and God took from them the day of their home-coming".

"It was a sweet view—sweet to the eye and to the mind, English verdure, English culture, English comfort, seen under a sun bright without being oppressive."[1]

"Ne rien outrer, ne rien affecter, plutôt rester un peu en deçà, ne point trop accuser la ligne ni le ton, voilà de quoi nous avons besoin d'être avertis." (As contrasted with—"tout ce qui force le ton, tout ce qui jure et crie, dans la couleur, dans le style, dans la pensée, dans l'observation et la description des objets extérieurs, dans les découvertes et les analyses à perte de vue qu'on prétend donner de la nature humaine, qui en déplacent violemment le centre, qui en bouleversent l'équilibre.")[2]

Heraclitus' "Dry light is best." The inscription in Madame Geoffrin's *salon*, "rien en relief".

> Truth sits upon the lips of dying men,
> And falsehood, while I lived, was far from mine.[3]

> To see life steadily and see it whole.[4]

> J'ai senti son beau corps tout froid entre mes bras.[5]

> Belle sans ornement, dans le simple appareil
> D'une beauté qu'on vient d'arracher au sommeil.[5]

---

[1] Jane Austen.
[2] Sainte-Beuve, *Étude sur Virgile*. Cf. his *Térence* in *Nouveaux Lundis*,v.
[3] Arnold, *Sohrab and Rustum*.   [4] Arnold, on Sophocles.
[5] Racine.

It was not God that gave me your commandment,
Nor Justice, consort of the Lords of Death,
That laid down *such* laws for the sons of men;
Nor did I hold that in your human edicts
Dwelt power to override the laws of God,
Unwritten, yet unshaken—laws that live
Not from to-day, nor yet from yesterday,
But always, though none knows how first made known.[1]

Fall'n Cherube, to be weak is miserable.[2]

Eyeless in Gaza at the mill with slaves.[2]

My thoughtless youth was wing'd with vain desires;
My manhood, long misled with wandering fires,
Follow'd false lights; and when their glimpse was gone,
My pride struck out new sparkles of her own.
Such was I, such by nature still I am;
Be Thine the glory, and be mine the shame.[3]

The Three Emperors were saintly men,
Yet to-day—where are they?
P'eng lived to a great age,
Yet he went at last, when he longed to stay.
And late or soon all go:
Wise and simple have no reprieve.
Wine may bring forgetfulness,
But does it not hasten old age?
If you set your heart on noble deeds,
How do you know that any will praise you?
By all this thinking you do Me injury:
You had better go where Fate leads—
Drift on the Stream of Infinite Flux
Without joy, without fear:
When you must go—then go
And make as little fuss as you can.[4]

---

[1] Sophocles, *Antigone*.   [2] Milton.   [3] Dryden.
[4] Tao Chien (A.D. 365–427: transl. by Arthur Waley). It is worth
noting that "Romantic" *motifs* like "the Three Emperors" and "the
Stream of Infinite Flux" hardly retain any glow of Romantic colour
or excitement in the grey light of this calm wisdom.

Émile Faguet's criticism on *Lear*: "Que me font toutes ces bêtes féroces? La porte de la ménagerie a été ouverte et voilà tout."

Homer's Greeks advancing in measured silence, while the Trojans and their Asian allies shout and scream like cranes in the windy heavens. Lord Chesterfield's refrain, "The graces, the graces!"

> Daughters of Zeus, you know what man's life is,
>   How brief, and yet how long the while—
> Its epics, falls of sparrows; its tragedies
>   Half farces and half vile;
> How every hero's sword at last grows brittle,
> How his dream fades, and night comes in a little—
>   And you smile.
>
> All else turns vanity: but yours the day
>   Of little things, that grow not less.
> Our moments fly—enough if on their way
>   You lent them loveliness.
> Alone of gods, you lie not; yours no Heaven
> That totters in the clouds—what you have given,
>   We possess.

Grace, self-knowledge, self-control; the sense of form, the easy wearing of the chains of art hidden under flowers, as with some sculptured group that fills with life and litheness its straitened prison in the triangle of a pediment; idealism steadied by an unfaltering sense of reality; lamp and midnight-oil, rather than wine-cup— these are the salient features here.[1] We may seem drifting

[1] I am of course using "Classical" throughout in the critical, not the historical, sense; with reference not to the "Classical" literature of Greece and Rome, some of which is highly Romantic, but to work which gives the same sort of feeling as the poetry of Sophocles, Horace, or Racine, the prose of Demosthenes or La Bruyère. A good example of the elusiveness of the whole distinction occurs in Professor Laurie Magnus's *Dict. of European Lit.*, *s.v.* "Romance", where of More's *Utopia*

back to the old antithesis: "Classicism—Romanticism, Reason—Emotion". But the human mind is more complex than that. What are the psychological differences behind these spontaneous associations of the two words?

Civilized man is pulled this way and that by conflicting forces within him, which it is the whole difficult art of life to reconcile. First, there are the instinctive impulses of the human animal; secondly, there are the influences of other human beings, beginning with his parents, which build up in him certain ideals of behaviour, a certain conscience about misbehaviour, till these too become second nature. A man not only likes or dislikes certain things; he likes or dislikes himself for liking or disliking them. Thirdly, his intelligence presents him a shadow-show of what he calls "reality". Meredith has symbolized these three as Blood (or the Dragon, or the Worm), Spirit, and Brain. Freud has more clearly pictured the unhappy lot of the "ego" torn three ways between the "id", the "super-ego", and the "reality-principle". It is no longer a case of "the world, the flesh, and the devil"; but of the world, the flesh, and the ideal.

it is remarked: "The form was classical, yet the matter was romantic. No scholar's Latinity could cloak the *chivalric* origin of the sentiments which More's hero 'had customably in his mouth': 'He that hath no grave, is covered with the sky', and 'the way to heaven out of all places is of like length and distance'. These sayings were penned by Thomas More in the elegant Latin of 1516, but they echoed the chivalric *roman* of the 12th cent. in Norman France." Curiously enough the first of these "romantic" quotations is simply the classic tag of Lucan—"Caelo tegitur qui non habet urnam"; and the second surely goes back to the classical sentiment, expressed in one of the epigrams of the Anthology (x, 3), that whether from Athens or from Meroë the road runs straight to Hades. Neither of these ideas strikes me as "Romantic"; but that may, of course, be due to having recognized their classical origin.

The instinctive, animal "id" moves under us towards some object of desire, as a horse we are sitting on towards a tuft of grass. But the tuft of grass may be growing on unattainable or forbidden ground. "It can't be done", cries the reality-principle; "it isn't done", whispers the super-ego. And the rider, the poor ego, tugs desperately at the rein.

Naturally the ego finds life hard in such a triangle of forces. To simplify things it has recourse to blinkers; not however for the horse, but for the rider—for itself. It shuts its eyes to certain impulses and conflicts too difficult to resolve; they are "repressed"; but they still go on writhing unconsciously, like Enceladus turning for ever on his bed of pain under Etna.

This is the essential thing that has been studied of late years—the vital importance of what goes on in our minds without our knowledge. Much of the Freudian system may be purest moonshine. There is no harm in being sceptical about it; on the contrary. It is, indeed, essential to say: "Things work *as if* this or that were the case— *as if* there were an unconscious 'id', a partly unconscious 'ego' and 'super-ego'". With all human theories, indeed, it is vital to hold hard to this as-ifery; then they may prove extremely helpful, without duping us. All theories are crutches, not sceptres or wizards' wands.

It seems, then, *as if* a great deal went on under the surface of our conscious lives. And when we sleep, it is as if the censor who keeps these ideas and impulses submerged, the jailer, Charon, or Cerberus of these ghosts, relaxed his vigilance; so that his prisoners can slip out and revisit the upper world—in our dreams.

But even then they come more or less disguised to enjoy this temporary release.

Sometimes, indeed, dreams seem staged by normally conscious impulses which merely invent for themselves an imaginary situation that allows the sleeper to go on sleeping. Sometimes, at least, this appears to be the actual purpose of dreaming. So that the starving explorer regularly dreams of banquets, as if to prevent his hunger from waking him. Or the exile sees his home—

> And we in dreams behold the Hebrides.[1]

Or again, the dream-disguise may be a far more impenetrable fancy-dress, with bizarre symbols that only analysis can strip to reveal the repressed impulse beneath.

Now the lives men live and the art they make depends, I think, enormously on how strict and oppressive, or relaxed and easygoing, are their sense of reality and their sense of the ideal, their consciousness and their conscience. Different periods vary widely in this—and, within periods, different individuals. It is as if some men loved (like D. H. Lawrence), and some even loathed (like Lord Chesterfield), the preconscious and instinctive side of personality. In each of us lies this dark lake from which our conscious, reasoning selves have gradually emerged; strange emanations dance by night, or at solitary moments, on its surface; still stranger shapes

[1] These isles, which have been such an abiding home for the Romantic imagination, from *Lycidas*, through Ossian and Collins and even Johnson, down to Wordsworth and the *Canadian Boat Song* and Poe, provide incidentally a supreme example of the inter-dependence of form and idea. Would they not have missed their poetic destiny, despite all their poetic scenery and legend, but for the happy error of some far-off scribe who first inserted in the tame correctness of "Ebudes" that echoing "r", the "litera canina"?

appear to inhabit its hidden depths. Some of us love to
dream on the banks of this mysterious mere; some try
to fish or dive in it; others labour to brick it over and blot
it out beneath a laboratory, or business-premises, or
a dancing-floor.

In art these differences are specially important
because there seems a good deal in common between all
artistic creation and dreaming. Mediaeval poets made
a habit of framing their poems in a setting of dream.
Stevenson has described his indebtedness to the marion-
ettes of sleep. Even the seemingly stolid Crabbe kept
writing materials by his bed; for "many a good bit",
so he told Lady Scott, came to him in dreams. Opium,
again, has given us *Kubla Khan*, *The Confessions of an
Opium-eater*, and Crabbe's *Sir Eustace Grey*. And even
those who rely only on their waking moments, know how
mysterious and capricious is the coming of good ideas
and how easily they slip away; so that Samuel Butler
found it necessary to keep note-books "to put salt on
their tails". Even the Classic Pope, most deliberate and
conscious of artists, would yet call up his amanuensis
time after time on freezing nights to secure on paper the
latest windfall of his brain. And as far back as the Classic
Dryden there is a foreshadowing of the working of the
unconscious mind, in his dedication of *The Rival Ladies*:
"This worthless present was designed you, long before
it was a play, when it was only a confused mass of
Thoughts, tumbling over one another in the dark; when
the Fancy was yet in its first work, moving the sleeping
images of things towards the light, there to be distinguished, and then either chosen or rejected by the Judg-
ment." And of this same process in the mind of Coleridge,

Professor Lowes has given a fascinating analysis in *The Road to Xanadu*. Idea after idea from Coleridge's reading or experience sinks into the reservoir of memory, to couple in the dark like unseen fish and produce strange hybrids that will one day leap back to the light—there to be caught and transferred, quivering with new life, to the Mariner's ocean or to the sacred stream of Kubla Khan. So considered, the differences between Classicism, Romanticism, and Realism turn out, I think, to be differences mainly of degree; depending on the strictness with which, if we may call them so, the reality-principle and the super-ego control and censor such emanations from the unconscious mind. The Realist writer tends to sacrifice everything to his sense of reality. The Classic, while ruthless towards some forms of unreality in the name of "good sense", elaborately cultivates others in the name of "good taste"; his impulses and fantasies are much more dominated by a social ideal, formed under the pressure of a finely civilized class.

Of the havoc too strong a sense of probability or of propriety can work with the imagination there remains no better example than Bentley's edition of Milton. Thus the poet writes—

> No light, but rather darkness visible.

If the darkness was visible, growls Bentley, how could "sights of woe" be visible through it? Read—

> No light, but rather a transpicuous gloom.

Milton's

> As from the centre thrice to the utmost pole

becomes with equally good reason—

> Distance which to express all measure fails.

And at the close of the whole poem, it will never do to say—

> They hand in hand with wandr'ing steps and slow
> Through Eden took their solitary way.

"Erratic steps? Very improper." They were being guided by Providence. And why "solitary"? They were no more solitary out of Eden than they had been in it. Therefore read—

> Then hand in hand with social steps their way
> Through Eden took, with Heav'nly comfort cheer'd.

Bentley's *Milton* is indeed a perfect monument of the too Classic mind. The Romantic side of the poet is what this pedant can least bear. It is precisely those passages that have become most famous that the Master of Trinity again and again picks out as spurious: such as the catalogue of cities ("from the destined Walls of Cambalu)"; the catalogue of serpents ("scorpions" are not serpents; and how can they hiss?); or, best of all, the catalogue of storied chivalry that "jousted at Aspramont or Montalban". This is "romantic trash". Even Proserpine "gathering flowers" and "carried off by gloomy Dis" is here carried off a second time by gloomier learning. But perhaps the finest example of such misplaced common sense is the treatment of Satan floating like Leviathan on the burning lake—

> So stretch'd out huge in length the Arch-fiend lay.

"That is improper; for the Whale cannot *stretch out* or contract any of his Joints; he is always of the same length."

By such intensive thought does literalism prevent whales, or poets, from adding cubits to their stature.

Johnson's objections to *Lycidas* show the same over-rigid sense of fact at work. "They had no flocks to batten." Whereas a Romantic like Mrs Radcliffe has no such qualms of pedantic honesty. *The Mysteries of Udolpho*, in defiance of all the astronomers since Ptolemy, can hardly admit a night without a moon. As soon as the sun sets, the more Romantic luminary is ruthlessly hauled above the horizon. Similarly Chateaubriand, describing to a friend an evening's journey, adds with a flash of candour: "Je sens bien que si la lune n'avait pas été là réellement, je l'aurais toujours mise dans ma lettre." Even the private letters of Romantics, it appears, cried for the moon.

The Romantic is in fact, like Joseph, a "dreamer". He may indeed, like a nightmare, be vividly realistic at moments. At moments he may be ruled, like the Classic, by a social ideal of conduct—partly social, at least, in its heroism and generosity, though in other ways rebelliously anti-social. But, essentially, he believes with Blake in letting his impulses and ideas run free—"Damn braces, bless relaxes"—"Exuberance is beauty".

> The Land of Dreams is better far
> Above the light of the morning-star.

Alcohol, I gather, does not so much stimulate the brain as relax its higher controls. Romanticism is likewise an intoxication; though there are varying degrees of it, just as there are day-dreams, night-dreams, nightmares, drink-dreams, and drug-dreams. If I had to hazard an Aristotelian definition of Romanticism, it might run— "Romantic literature is a dream-picture of life; providing sustenance and fulfilment for impulses cramped by society or reality".

Whereas the world of Classicism, on the contrary, is wide awake and strictly sober. For Lord Chesterfield, writing to his son, the unpardonable sin in good society is to let the mind wander. For Johnson, the theatre remains always a theatre—he does not talk, like Coleridge, of "suspending his disbelief". Even for Diderot, the good actor always remembers he is an actor. Classical French drama stands at attention, formal as a grenadier. "Monsieur Macbeth, prenez bien garde à Monsieur Macduff." The passions of Racine depend on none of that riot of realistic local colóur and fantastic passion adored by the Romantics. When Boswell says certain music makes him want to rush into the thick of the fight, like an avalanche descends the inexorable snub—"I should never hear it, if it made me such a fool". Not because Johnson was anti-militarist; on the contrary, he has observed that all men are secretly ashamed of not being soldiers. Not because Johnson lacked passion; we know better. But even on his death-bed, with all his horror of death, he would have his clear-headedness clouded with no narcotics. And here poor Boswell with his martial ardours was being silly. That was the supremely forbidden thing; one must not be silly. He was getting drunk; and gentlemen should carry their liquor. "Things and actions are what they are," comes the calm, firm voice of the eighteenth century through the lips of Bishop Butler, "and the consequences of them will be what they will be; why then should we desire to be deceived?"[1]

[1] Cf. Mme de Staal-Delaunay's briefer "Le vrai est comme il peut et n'a de mérite que d'être ce qu'il est."

Why? Precisely for that very reason. Things as they
are leave so much to be desired. "I am never better",
cries Hieronimo in the *Spanish Tragedy* "than when I am
mad; then methinks I am a brave fellow; then I do
wonders; but reason abuseth me, and there's the torment,
there's the hell." Rousseau dreams all day long, like
a fakir, in his little boat on the Lake of Bienne. The
works of Chateaubriand are the endless melancholy
reverie of a figure dreaming with folded arms on the
St Helena of his lonely egotism. "Eh!" he cries, too
histrionically, "Eh! qui n'a passé des heures entières
assis sur le rivage d'un fleuve, à voir s'écouler les ondes?"
Why, a great many people. Imagine Dr Johnson's
contemptuous reply to such an idle question. But for
René a dream is the richest legacy he can leave his own
child. "Qu'on ne parle jamais de moi à ma fille," he
writes to his Indian maiden, Céluta, "que René reste
pour elle un homme inconnu, dont l'étrange destin[1]
raconté la fasse rêver sans qu'elle en pénètre la cause;
je ne veux être à ses yeux que ce que je suis, un pénible
songe." "Les rêves", writes the Romantic Charles
Nodier, "sont ce qu'il y a de plus doux et peut-être de
plus vrai dans la vie." This refrain, *rêve, rêver, rêverie,*
seems to echo from page to page of French Romanticism
—*c'est une rêve sans trêve.*

Similarly in England, at the very gateway of the
Revival, Horace Walpole's *Castle of Otranto* is built out of
a dream and written half in one.[2] "Visions, you know",
writes its wise and charming author, whose memory,

---

[1] Cf. p. 103, footnote. One thinks too of Byron and Ada.

[2] On a later visit to Cambridge, Walpole suddenly recognized in
the court of a College the model used by his unconscious memory to
build his Castle in Italy.

for some reason, critics treat so disdainfully, "have always been my pasture; and so far from growing old enough to quarrel with their emptiness, I almost think there is no wisdom comparable to that of exchanging what is called the realities of life for dreams. Old castles, old pictures, old histories, and the babble of old people, make one live back into centuries that cannot disappoint one. The dead have exhausted their power of deceiving— one can trust Catherine of Medicis now." Macpherson's *Ossian* is a monotonous dream of shadows. "Dream not, Coleridge," cries Lamb, "of having tasted all the grandeur and wildness of fancy till you have gone mad." "You never dream", says Coleridge in his turn reproach-fully to Hazlitt. And again: "I should much wish, like the Indian Vishnu, to float about along an infinite ocean, cradled in the flower of the Lotus, and wake once in a million years for a few minutes just to know that I was going to sleep a million years more". Even as a boy, seized in the street by a gentleman for picking his pocket, he turned out to have been merely waving his hands in a day-dream that he was Leander swim-ming the Hellespont to Hero's tower. In later years his dreams became less pleasant; the creator of *Kubla Khan* fled through much of his life like the figure in his *Ancient Mariner* who hears the stalking footsteps of a fiend behind. "Dreams with me are no Shadows, but the very Substances and foot-thick Calamities of my Life." And after him in the long pageant of Romantic dreamers follows de Quincey with his opium; Beddoes the "Dream-Pedlar"; Keats, "a dreaming thing, A fever of thyself", whose *La Belle Dame* arose from a dream of Dante's Francesca, and

whose *Endymion* de Quincey found, with some justice,
vaguer "than the reveries of an oyster"; Shelley beating
his wings high above the clouds; Byron,[1] whose *Dream*
is among his still living poems, and who slept with pistol
under pillow to ward off the too real phantoms of the
night; Clare turning back to refuge in madness from
"the living sea of waking dreams"; Tennyson hypnotizing himself into strange trances by the repetition of his
own name; Browning with his visionary visit to Childe

---

[1] Cf. Peacock's parody of Byron, Mr Cypress, to whom Mr Hilary
observes: "You talk like a Rosicrucian, who will love nothing but
a sylph, who does not believe in the existence of a sylph, and who yet
quarrels with the whole Universe for not containing a sylph." Peacock
wrote even more wisely than he knew. Chateaubriand has told in the
Memoirs published long after Peacock wrote, how in his young years at
Combourg he too lived through a long dream-romance with an imaginary
sylphide. Similarly Shelley's poet, in *Prometheus*:

> Nor seeks nor finds he mortal blisses
> But feeds on the aërial kisses
> Of shapes that haunt love's wildernesses.

We have travelled far here (too far, some will find) from the robust,
if cynical, Epicureanism of a Classic like Congreve—

> You think she's false, I'm sure she's kind,
> I'll take her body, you her mind.
>   Who has better bargain?

And yet, so important is a sane sense of reality in life, one may well
doubt if the realistic Congreve gave as much pain to those who loved
him as the idealistic Shelley.

Contrast too that most typically eighteenth-century summary of life,
so sadly sane, addressed by Walpole to Mme du Deffand: "Rendez-vous
à la raison, prends le monde comme il est; n'attendez pas à le refaire
à votre gré, et ne ressemblez pas à ce prince dans les contes persans qui
courait le monde pour trouver une princesse qui ressemblât à certain
portrait qu'il avait vu au trésor de son père, et qui se trouve avoir été
la maîtresse de Salomon".

Roland's tower; Poe with his stud of speckled nightmares—

> And all my days are trances,
> And all my nightly dreams
> Are where thy dark eye glances,
> And where thy footstep gleams—
> In what ethereal dances!
> By what eternal streams!

Here too paces Rossetti,

> Master of the murmuring courts
> Where the shapes of sleep convene—

till sleeplessness and chloral mastered him; his sister
Christina,

> Dreaming through the twilight
> That does not rise nor set;

Morris following to the World's End, like his own Phara-
mond, the beauty seen and loved in dream; Francis
Thompson, dallying with his opium amid labouring
London, like the idle poppy amid the wheat—

> My fruit is dreams, as theirs is bread;

the languid O'Shaughnessy, the languider Dowson; de
la Mare "crazed with the spell of far Arabia", Yeats in
his Celtic twilight; and so to the *Surréalistes*, whose
principle it is to write not merely of dreams, or after
dreaming, but in one.

Not only did the Romantics prefer to create their art
in this atmosphere of dream. Even the critical power of
appreciating art seemed to Stendhal something only
to be acquired by a habit "de rêverie un peu mélan-
colique". Even history, not altogether to its advantage,
became in Romantic hands a dream likewise. "*L'Histoire*

de France de Michelet", says Heine[1] (in a passage that I came upon only after the rest of this was written), "est ce recueil de rêves, c'est tout le moyen âge rêveur qui vous regarde de ses yeux profonds, douloureux, avec son sourire de spectre, et l'on est presque effrayé par la criante vérité de la couleur et des formes. En fait, pour la peinture de cette époque somnambule, il fallait précisément un historien somnambule comme Michelet." Less Romantic critics will be more critical of this Romanticized history; but the passage well brings out the persistent connection between the Middle Ages, Romanticism, and dream. Even autobiography proved too real a form for Romantics to write correctly.[2] Even their own past lives danced in a coloured mist before their eyes. But the clearest manifesto of this side of Romantic dream-life, of the flight from reality, remains Baudelaire's.

Il faut être toujours ivre. Tout est là; c'est l'unique question.... Mais de quoi? De vin, de poésie, ou de vertu, à votre guise. Mais enivrez-vous.

Et si quelquefois, sur les marchés d'un palais, sur l'herbe verte d'un fossé, dans la solitude morne de votre chambre, vous vous réveillez, l'ivresse déjà diminuée ou disparue, demandez au vent, à la vague, à l'étoile, à l'oiseau, à l'horloge, à tout ce qui fuit, à tout ce qui gémit, à tout ce qui roule, à tout ce qui chante, à tout ce qui parle, demandez quelle heure il est; et le vent, la vague, l'étoile, l'oiseau, l'horloge, vous répondront: "Il est l'heure de s'enivrer! Pour n'être pas les esclaves martyrisés du Temps, enivrez-vous; enivrez-vous sans cesse! De vin, de poésie, ou de vertu, à votre guise."

---

[1] See Lasserre, *Le Romantisme Français*, p. 387.

[2] Cf. the vagaries of Chateaubriand and Coleridge in their reminiscences and Sainte-Beuve's scathing criticism of Lamartine's *Confidences* in *Causeries du Lundi*, 1.

Romanticism, in a word, was the Sleeping Beauty dreaming of the Fairy Prince; unfortunately the Fairy Prince is apt to lose his way; and the Sleeping Beauty may then console herself with other spirits that come, like the Arabian kind, out of bottles, but end all too unromantically in *delirium tremens*.

The eighteenth century had always had at its ear two voices, like the warning Daemon of Socrates; one whispering "That is not intelligent", the other, "That is not done". Romanticism seems to me, essentially, an attempt to drown these two voices and liberate the unconscious life from their tyrannical repressions. Like the accompanying French Revolution, it is the insurrection of a submerged population; but, this time, a population of the mind. "*Fancy*," remarked Rymer, the orthodox neo-Classic, "*Fancy* leaps and frisks and away she's gone, whilst *Reason* rattles the chains and follows after." Now at last those chains were broken; the Bastille of those twin oppressors, Probability and Propriety, was stormed and obliterated. In this sense, indeed, "Le Romantisme, c'est la Révolution".[1]

The views of writers themselves on the actual business of composition help to confirm this, by differing significantly, according as they are more Classical or Romantic. The Romantic, depending more on processes outside his conscious control, believes, like Plato, in "inspiration"

---

[1] Jung, with his idea of the collective Unconscious, would possibly put it that the sensitive minds of poets and artists now became aware that an essential part of human nature was being starved. But this seems only a rather mystical way of saying that healthy instincts first reasserted themselves in certain more imaginative personalities; because these artists were more sensitive, they felt more distinctly where their shoes pinched.

or "furor poeticus", a divine drunkenness. Whereas Davenant, at the dawn of neo-Classicism, already sniffs at this idea. It is, for him, a relic of the primitive days when poets, being also priests, were of course charlatans, who found it politic to pretend to be possessed. Poets, he holds, should be "painful", even if they are abused for lack of fury. And painful indeed Davenant and his successors often contrived to be. For Pope, again, the cool, conscious, critical judgement is so important, that he keeps his poems for two years before publishing them; less exacting in this than Horace who demanded nine. The Classic Johnson, with his bitter Grub Street experience, finds it foppery in Gray and Milton to depend on moods or seasons and insists that a man can *always* write who sets himself "doggedly" to it; Trollope, that healthy realist, proved it for himself by turning out his thousand words an hour with the precision of a sausage-machine—much to the disgust of the British public, when he revealed it. For the British public cherished far more Romantic ideas of inspiration. Balzac, again, who soon turned from Romance to Realism, condemns as fatal for writers the romantic reverie, which he calls "smoking enchanted cigarettes". He himself preferred to write eighteen hours a day on black coffee.

But Ronsard had possessed no such self-control.

> Poète je suis
> Plein de fureur; car faire je ne puis
> Un trait de vers, soit qu'un prince commande,
> Soit qu'une dame ou l'ami m'en demande,
> Et à tous coups la verve ne me prend:
> Je bée en vain, et mon esprit attend
> Tantost six mois, tantost un an sans faire
> Vers qui me puisse ou plaire ou satisfaire.

For Wordsworth poetry is "the *spontaneous* overflow of powerful feelings". Burns owned that he had always failed when, twice or thrice, he had tried to force himself. Professor Housman in our own day has illustrated this importance of the Unconscious in poetry. In his own experience slightly bad health was a help.[1] (I have found the impulse similarly heightened by unhappiness—just as discomfort in sleep may stimulate us to dream.) He would take a pint of beer at lunch and a walk in the afternoon, his least intellectual time of day. Lines or even stanzas would bubble up, as from the pit of the stomach; together with a vague idea of the poem as a whole. Later, a return of inspiration might fill up the gaps; or this might have to be done by "the brain". Thus two stanzas of a poem came on Hampstead Heath; a third "with a little coaxing after tea"; the fourth had to be written thirteen times over and took a whole twelvemonth.

Other Romantics, however, have been able to write and dream with extraordinary facility; just as some people can go to sleep the moment their heads touch the pillow, or even hypnotize themselves. George Sand is said to have finished one novel at 2 a.m., then taken a fresh sheet and started another. Byron could compose while dressing for balls; Morris once turned out seven hundred verses in a day. But it is symptomatic that they both hated correcting. Like Shakespeare, who never blotted a line, and Scott, who could send manuscripts to the printer without re-reading them, Byron refused to revise, or even to believe that any gain could come of it. "I am like a tiger: if I miss my first spring, I go grumbling

[1] Cf. p. 8.

back to my jungle." So too Morris preferred to rewrite where necessary, rather than polish. The explanation is, I imagine, that the critical wakefulness of revision is the extreme opposite of a creative semi-trance; and even writers who can induce the trance quite easily, find it hard to combine with the vigilant mood of self-criticism.

Other Romantics, however, seem able even to do this: the manuscript of *Atalanta in Calydon* is covered with corrections; and Rossetti irritated even Swinburne by his endless second thoughts.

From all this it is clearly hard to generalize. But I believe that though Romantic writers are often by no means (as they say of fruit-trees) "shy bearers", still "shy bearers" have generally Romantic tendencies—like Coleridge and Housman. It would surprise me to find many really Classical writers so dependent on "inspiration"—on processes quite beyond conscious control. Indeed their control is often too conscious: such presence of mind may mean absence of poetry. In a word the typical Romantic, I believe, tends to be either distinctly prolific, like Hugo, or distinctly costive, like Coleridge, at least so far as good work is concerned: the typical Classic is less likely, in this also, to reach extremes. He is often able to write by simply willing it; but, being more self-critical, less ready to write anyhow.

At all events, whereas the diverse theories of Romanticism quoted earlier seemed one-sided—each like a single photograph of a building taken from a different aspect—it now becomes possible, I think, to assemble them as parts of a more intelligible whole.

Thus Romanticism is not, in Goethe's phrase, "disease". It is intoxicated dreaming. But it is easy to see, and we shall see, that such auto-intoxication can often become the reverse of healthy.

Again, Romanticism is not simply a revolt of Emotion against Reason, though it often is; nor yet of Imagination against Reason—a "renascence of Wonder"; it can be both of these, or either. As there are two tyrants to rebel against—the sense of reality and the sense of society, the rebellion may be highly imaginative yet not very passionate, like much of Coleridge; or passionate yet not highly imaginative, like much of Byron; or both, like *Adonais*.

That rules like the Unities should be among the first things to be flung aside by Romanticism, follows naturally. For it is hard to dream in a stiff shirt-front; and exhilarated revellers dislike being asked to toe chalk lines on the floor. Far better Herrick's "wild civility" or, as Musset writes of Régnier—

> tes beaux vers ingénus,
> Tantôt légers, tantôt boiteux, toujours pieds nus.[1]

And so Romanticism, in order that it may be free to dream, becomes a literary Protestantism, Liberalism, or rule of *laissez-faire*.

Again, the Middle Ages were its obvious spiritual home. For they were mystical, mysterious, and remote; and they had been finally killed at the Renaissance by this hated Classicism, which the Romantics now pro-

---

[1] Cf. Francis Thompson:

> We speak a lesson taught we know not how,
> And what it is that from us flows,
> The hearer better than the utterer knows.

posed to kill in its turn. But the mediaeval is no essential part of the Romantic.

Finally, Romanticism is only partly opposed to Realism; its true enemy is the hackneyed and humdrum present, whether squalid or academic—a very different thing. Snatches of realism remain very welcome to Romantic sensationalists, especially as an escape from the starched dignities of Classicism; just as a courtier of the old régime used, he said, on returning from the pomps of Versailles, to stand and stare at a dog gnawing a bone in the street—here at last was something "real".

Thus Romantic diction shows fondness not only for the romantically remote, in place or time, but also for the realistic. While Coleridge, Keats, and Morris revived words long hoary and moss-grown, Wordsworth, on the contrary, copied the actual speech of "huts where poor men lie" and Hugo boasted that he had stuck a red cap of liberty on the Dictionary of the Academy.

Further, from its relaxation of the censorship over the Unconscious or the Preconscious, follow naturally certain other features of Romantic literature.

We have become familiar with the enormous part played by symbolism in all dreaming. It plays an enormous part also in enriching the imagery of this "literature of dream". Dryden with his Classicism had already found Shakespeare's style "pestered" with figurative expressions. Aristotle and Longinus would certainly have shuddered at his extravagances. But with the Romantic Revival, after the hackneyed metaphors and similes of neo-Classicism, appeared a new wealth of images, often as grotesque and fantastic as a dream,

which would have seemed to Boileau or Johnson, in the
phrase of Beddoes—

> like a satyr grinning in a brook
> To find Narcissus' round and downy face.

Half a century later these two attitudes could still
clash. The young Parnassians had asked Hugo for a letter
of approval to serve as preface to *Le Parnasse Contemporain*.
In reply,

> Verbosa et grandis epistola venit
> A Capreis—

or rather from Guernsey. According to Anatole France,
it began: "Jeunes gens, je suis le passé: vous êtes l'avenir.
Je ne suis qu'une feuille: vous êtes la forêt. Je ne suis
qu'une chandelle: vous êtes les rayons de soleil. Je ne
suis qu'un bœuf: vous êtes les rois mages." And so on
for four pages. A practical joke was suspected. No, it
was deadly earnest. They decided to do without this too
similitudinous benediction.[1]

Again the Romantic writers use language in a dreamier
way; with vague overtones and associations that shall
echo through a mind whose attention is not riveted but
half relaxed.

> I know not whether
> I see your meaning; if I do, it lies
> Upon the wordy wavelets of your voice
> Dim as the evening shadow in a brook,
> When the least moon has silver on't no larger
> Than the pure white of Hebe's pinkish nail.[2]

> Such was his weapon, and he traced with it
> Upon the waters of my thoughts, these words:
> "I am the death of flowers and nightingales
> And small-lipped babes, that give their souls to summer

---

[1] See Souriau, *Hist. du Romantisme*, II, 294.   [2] Beddoes.

To make a perfumed day with: I shall come,
A death no larger than a sigh to thee
Upon a sunset hour." And so he passed
Into the place where faded rainbows are,
Dying along the distance of my mind.[1]

Such thoughts are themselves like shadows in water;
such phrases like the water's drowsy lullaby. In the
Romantic hands that thus "writ in water", other words
besides Keats's "forlorn" grow "like a bell"; indeed
a Romantic sentence is often a whole carillon of such bells,
an Easter chime that calls the ghosts of forgotten meanings
to rise again.

> The fairy fancies range
> And, lightly stirr'd,
> Ring little bells of change
> From word to word.[2]

We are far here from the days

> When *Phoebus* touch'd the Poet's trembling Ear
> With one supreme Commandment: "Be thou clear".[3]

How blind by contrast the eighteenth century could
be to the dreamy associations of words is well seen in an
astonishing passage by the Abbé de Pons (1714), vindi-
cating his right to judge Homer without even knowing
Greek:[4] "Chaque nation a ses signes fixes pour repré-
senter tous les objets que son intelligence embrasse.
Qu'on ne dise donc plus que les beautés qu'on a senties
en lisant Homère ne peuvent être parfaitement rendues
en français. Ce qu'on a senti ou pensé, on peut l'exprimer
avec une élégance *égale* dans toutes les langues." To
this good Abbé words are merely like algebraic symbols;
his mind concentrates on the barest literal meaning;

---

[1] Beddoes.   [2] Tennyson.   [3] Austin Dobson.
[4] See Sainte-Beuve, *Causeries du Lundi*, XIII, 154.

to let it wander away to half-conscious associations would be reprehensible wool-gathering. He did not guess that such wool might be the Golden Fleece of poetry. These neo-Classics were not emotionally over-cold, but mentally over-alert; not unfeeling, but unsleeping.

So with metre. The essential difference between Romantic verse, in England and France, and the immaculate heroics and Alexandrines of the Classics is that rhythm has now become once more an intoxicant. "Enivrez-vous!" Pope or Gray, Racine or Boileau can speak perfectly; they can declaim magnificently; but they do not sing. Their verse is exquisite coffee in lordly porcelain; it "cheers but not inebriates"; it is not the wine of Dionysus. It hardly performs at all the essential task of more dancing rhythms—the task of hypnotizing the reader into a dreamy trance, where his sense of reality is drugged and, at the same time, his suggestibility heightened. The music of Handel, Gluck, and Mozart (such a complete refutation of the supposed passionlessness of the eighteenth century) failed to infect the sister-art of poetry. In literature, for a century and a half Apollo had harped with a dignity sometimes splendid, often monotonous; now at last the wild flutings of Marsyas were once more to catch at the heart and go shuddering down the spine.

> With throats unslaked, with black lips baked,
>   Agape they heard me call.

> My ornaments are arms,
>   My pastime is in war,
> My bed is cold upon the wold,
>   My lamp yon star.[1]

[1] Lockhart.

Tirra, lirra, by the river
  Sang Sir Lancelot.

And the Witch stepped down from her casement.
  In the hush of night he heard
The calling and wailing in dewy thicket
  Of bird to hidden bird.[1]

The old mayor climbed the belfry tower,
  The ringers ran by two, by three:
"Pull, if ye never pulled before,
  Good ringers, pull your best," quoth he.
"Play uppe, play uppe, O Boston Bells!
  Play all your changes, all your swells,
  Play uppe the Brides of Enderby!"[2]

Beau cavalier, qui partez pour la guerre,
Qu'allez-vous faire
Si loin d'ici?
Voyez-vous pas que la nuit est profonde
Et que le monde
N'est que souci?[3]

Far the calling bugles hollo,
  High the screaming fife replies,
Gay the files of scarlet follow.
  Woman bore me, I will rise.[4]

To-day knights-errant are rust and dust, witches ashes, war a folly; but as the trees with Orpheus, so to such music we can still forget our most stiffly rooted convictions. It was not for nothing that in a realistic moment Shelley compared himself for unreality to a gin-palace. Intoxication is the essence of such poetry as this.

So with Romantic settings and subject-matter. Always "la princesse lointaine", the blue of distance. For

[1] Walter de la Mare.   [2] Jean Ingelow.
[3] Alfred de Musset.   [4] Housman.

remoteness is a feeling associated with dreams; and, again, remoteness makes it easier to dream—there is less danger of colliding with a brute fact. It may be remoteness in time—

> When the last bubbles of Atlantis broke
> Among the quieting of its heaving floor.[1]

> Very old are the woods
>   And the buds that break
> Out of the briar's boughs
>   When March winds wake,
> So old with their beauty are—
>   Oh no man knows
> Through what wild centuries
>   Roves back the rose.[2]

Or it may be remoteness in space, as with Heine's fir-tree—the distance of far Arabia or Xanadu, of Tipperary or "the lands where the Jumblies live".

> Distance presents the object fair
> With Charming features and a graceful Air,
> But when we come to seize th' inviting prey,
> Like a Shy Ghost, it vanishes away.

> The distance lends enchantment to the view
> And robes the mountain in its azure hue.[3]

Or, again, it may be that other remoteness of undiscovered countries of the mind. "Who", says Fuller, "hath sailed about the world of his own heart, sounded each creek, surveyed each corner, but that there still remains much *terra incognita* in himself?"

The Romantics found this *terra incognita* of the soul their happy hunting ground. And yet dreamers may

---

[1] Gordon Bottomley.   [2] Walter de la Mare.
[3] Norris of Bemerton and Campbell (quoted in Abercrombie. *Romanticism*).

not make the best explorers; the results, as we shall see, were not always very happy. "Enfin on est attristé, en même temps qu'effrayé", writes Anatole France of Hugo, "de ne pas rencontrer dans son œuvre énorme, au milieu de tant de monstres, une seule figure humaine." Hugo is an extreme, but not an isolated case. It is the passionate personality of these writers, the intensity of their atmosphere, that makes their real strength. "I have no pity, I have no pity! The more the worms writhe, the more I yearn to crush out their entrails. It is a moral teething; and I grind with greater energy in proportion to the increase of pain.... He gnashed at me, and foamed like a mad dog, and gathered her to him with greedy jealousy...his sharp cannibal teeth...his basilisk eyes" —these things do not come from some tenth-rate novelette: they are from *Wuthering Heights*, which remains a masterpiece in spite of such Satanic crudities.

Similarly in other fields where more conscious critical control is needed—in the construction of a plot, in the creation of a *prose* style—the Romantic in his semi-trance is often inferior to the century before. Then, a gentleman regarded his readers as his guests. He considered it his duty to face the toil of hard writing in order to give them the pleasure of easy reading; unlike Mr Joyce who has touchingly remarked "The demand that I make of my reader is that he should devote his whole life to reading my works". Of the more serious weaknesses which come from the Romantic surrender to impulse it will be time to speak when we deal with its decadence.

These, then, seem to me the essential effects of the wine of Romanticism. Naturally they vary enormously with the strength of the dose. One glass will quicken a man's intelligence and observation; a dozen will undermine them. "Dry light is best"; but too dry a life may not be— at least in matters of the imagination. The eighteenth century carried dryness to excess. The Romantic reaction was healthy; but, like most reactions, it became extravagant and so unhealthy in its turn. The Romantic writer, squeezing "Joy's grape" against his palate, grows more eloquent, more magical in the music of phrase and imagery, more impressive in the frank intensity of his feeling and imagination, in the atmosphere that only passion can create. He can be a bewitching companion. But he loses more and more, as his intoxication increases, the balance, the proportion, the control, the power to coordinate, of the great masters; the intelligence and grace of the man of the world; the quiet sympathy a writer needs in order to observe and delineate characters other than his own or shadows of his own—that exaggerated ego which in the Romantics often grows as bloated as an ant-queen among her crawling subjects; fertile, but grotesque. Such, for better and for worse, seem to me the symptoms of Romanticism, this dream-gift of Dionysus, who brings release for the soul in chains, but for those that follow him too far, new chains heavier still; who has wrecked life after life, and yet immeasurably enriched the world.

CHAPTER II

THE CROCODILES OF ALACHUA;
OR THE PAST OF ROMANTICISM

THE essential difference, it has so far been suggested, between Classicism and Romanticism is that the control exerted by the conscious mind, particularly by the sense of reality and the sense of society, is strict in the first—while in the second it is relaxed, somewhat as in drunkenness or dream. The words "Classic" and "Romantic" have, indeed, become so worn, smudged, and ambiguous that it might be wiser to invent new terms altogether. We might speak of "hyparistic" and "oneiristic" writing, from the Greek words for "waking" and "dream". But such words are horrible, if they can possibly be avoided; further, the description of Romantic literature as simply "dream-work" does not quite suffice. Except in its extreme forms, it does usually retain a super-ego, an ideal of conduct, of its own; often a highly quixotic one. But first it is worth looking back to earlier literature for examples of the "romantic" in its widest sense in order to test and check this theory of its nature. By "romantic", I mean, as has been said, things that give the same general feeling, of dream-life, as *La Belle Dame Sans Merci* or *The Ancient Mariner* or *The Haystack in the Floods*.

Romanticism is indeed as old as European literature—as old as the *Odyssey*. It is even older—there were geniuses before Homer. They are nameless now and forgotten, but their work remains; so much a part, still, of our lives that we take its existence for granted, like rain or sunlight, and fail to realize what gifts of imagination must have gone to create those legends of Greek mythology which no other race has ever equalled—not even the race of Cuchulain and the Celtic Twilight, nor the race of Sigurd and the Twilight of the Gods. It is the fancy of prehistoric Greeks that has turned our heavens to a constellated tapestry of the stories of Orion and Andromeda and the rest; that has planted our earth with flowers "inscripti nomine regum"—memorials of ill-starred youth and maid, like narcissus and hyacinth, the sunflower of Clytie and the anemone of Adonis. But this earlier Hellas shows one striking contrast to the later Greece of Sophocles and Thucydides. It breathes a fragrance of young romance which was one day to intoxicate Keats, even when he found its blossoms pressed and dry in the *hortus siccus* of Lemprière. Its legends turn, again and again, on that romantic passion which Aristophanes admired Aeschylus for ignoring and reviled Euripides for portraying. Here, too, magic transformations and many-headed monsters, all the fauna and flora of fairyland, luxuriate as freely as in Ariosto, or *The Arabian Nights*. In fact, few things are more romantic than "classical" mythology.

True, even in this romantic childhood the Greek sense of reality is already alive and awake; there is already a guardian set at the portal of this early dream-world to turn back shapes too fantastic. "Gorgons and hydras and chimaeras dire" may pass, to take their permanent place in the best European society; even oddities like the Graiai, those three old women sharing one eye and one tooth between them, who might suitably figure in a Communist's nightmare, manage to scrape by. But nothing is allowed here like the hyperbolic hero of Indian epic who stops the ten thousand arrows of a hostile army in mid-air by as many discharged from his own bow, or the daring extravagances of the Celtic imagination. The Greek Lynceus may see through wood or stone; but there is nothing like MacRoth, the spy of Maeve, as described in James Stephens's *Deirdre*: "He would spy in a bee-hive; he would spy on the horned end of the moon; he would spy in the middle of the sea, and would know which wave it was that drowned him and which wave it was that urged it."

Still, Greek mythology remains genuinely romantic. It is worth noting, too, the reappearance here of other familiar symptoms of Romanticism—incest and rebellion against the Father-God, as seen in the stories of Zeus and Hera, of the children of Aeolus, of Myrrha, Phaedra, and Jocasta; or in the mutilation of Ouranos by his insurgent son Cronos, who is dethroned by *his* son Zeus, who would have been overpowered in turn by *his* son, had he not refrained from the love of Thetis. Indeed, Greek legend has provided the name for that corner-stone of Freudianism, the Oedipus-complex itself.

But the actual literature of Greece already shows itself more self-disciplined. Homer, indeed, sometimes dreams; and was therefore accused of "nodding". "The dreams of Zeus"—so an ancient critic, disapproving yet admiring, describes the Romantic elements of the *Odyssey*. This writer, the so-called "Longinus", whose treatise *On Great Writing* probably belongs to the first century of the Roman Empire, shows most interestingly the inhibitions of the honest "Classical" mind. His sensitive sympathy recognizes that great writing should

bring intoxication, not information; yet he is genuinely
jarred by anything at all fantastic—"this will never do".
Even a lovely metaphor like Plato's description of his
unfortified Utopia—"the walls of our city shall be
suffered to sleep in the earth"—is too loud for him;
just as Aristotle had found the metaphor that the
Odyssey "held the mirror up to nature" strained and
unnatural. And when he is faced with the miracles of
the *Odyssey*, "Longinus" becomes, like so many Classics,
quite superstitiously unsuperstitious. He is afraid of
fairies just because they do *not* exist.

> All is bot gaistis and elriche fantasies,
> Of browneis and bogillis full this buke—

so Gavin Douglas was one day to write in delighted
praise at the beginning of his version of Virgil's Sixth
Book: such power had the mediaeval mind to throw
its many-coloured glamour even over the grey purity
of the classical Netherworld. But for "Longinus"
"browneis and bogillis" are highly suspect company.
"In the *Odyssey*," he writes, "Homer is like the setting
sun, less vigorous, not less great....As if Ocean were
ebbing back into the lonely isolation of his own confines,[1]
so the poet's greatness is here receding and he winds his
way among things fabulous and fantastic. In saying this,
I am not forgetting the storm-scenes of the *Odyssey* and
the episode of Polyphemus" (it is interesting that he
could swallow Polyphemus) "and certain other passages;
none the less we are faced with a writer weakened by
old age, though it still remains the old age of Homer.
Throughout the poem the fabulous does predominate

[1] The ebbing tide leaves monsters stranded behind it.

over the real. And I point this out to show how easily failing genius lapses into the ludicrous—into things like the shutting of the winds in a bag, or Circe's turning of men into swine—'squealing porkers', as Zoilus called them...." Zoilus, "the Homer-scourge", had been an earlier critic of Alexandria; and it is amusing to find the same sort of unimaginative cavil recurring two thousand years later on the Classic lips of Lord Chesterfield. Achilles, he observes, "wore the strongest armour in the world, which I humbly apprehend to be a blunder, for a horse-shoe clapped to his vulnerable heel would have been sufficient". The blunder is really his lordship's, for the legend of the hero's vulnerable heel was unknown to Homer. But how over-wakeful and over-sober, here as always, is the Classic sense of fact! When in the Laestrygonian land, with its fjord pale under the midnight sun, the comrades of Odysseus enter the hall of King Antiphates, they find his queen—some ancestress of Brynhild?—beside her hearth. "She was tall as a mountain-crag; and they hated her." Well, they might; in a moment they were to be eaten; but they did not hate such disproportion more intensely than Classic critics.

Plato blamed Homer because his gods were too immoral; Alexandria blamed him because his young ladies were too free; "Longinus", because his marvels were too incredible; Perrault, and such neo-Classics, because his manners were too real, his heroes too hail-fellow-well-met with swineherds. Throughout the history of criticism again and again these three aberrations recur—priggery, snobbery and over-realism.

But Homer is by no means the last Greek Romantic. "Longinus" and his like were similarly torn between enthusiasm and disapproval over Aeschylus. A giant in his own generation, he jarred on posterity; he was too like Isaiah or Marlowe. Just as men said Homer nodded and dreamed, the rumour went that Aeschylus dipped his pen in the wine-pot. His imagery was so undisciplined. He roared like a bull, they said, piled up phrases like towers, talked mountains. "A slippery, lonely-hearted, eagle-haunted crag, that towers sheer beyond the leap of goat, the gaze of man"—that phrase of his *Suppliants* is a fit symbol of the poet himself. He too remained a "lonely-hearted crag"—(how many other Greek writers would have used that epithet?)—remote from the ways of common men; until far away in his Sicilian exile, as legend told, an eagle dropped a tortoise on him, thinking the old man's head in truth a stone. Aeschylus formed in his own image, we feel (as Milton with Satan), that rebellious Titan chained to his crag near the North Pole, who so fired the imagination of Romantics like Shelley and Byron;[1] who turns from the cruelty of destiny, almost like Wordsworth, to Nature's silent witness;[2] whose imagination ranges like Marlowe's among the echoing names of the far countries of the world—

> Then take the Southward road
> Till you meet the army of the Amazons,
> Haters of men, that shall find their home hereafter
> In Themiscyra, by Thermōdon's stream,
> Where the jaw of Salmydessus cleaves the sea—
> Sour host to sailors, step-mother of ships.

[1] Cf. *Manfred*. Byron speaks of the *Prometheus* as being "so much in my head that I can easily conceive its influence on all or anything that I have ever written".

[2] Cf. the imaginative fancy preserved by Hyginus, that Prometheus knew the future because in the silence of the lonely nights he had overheard the singing of the Fates.

What imagery! Little wonder that from the fourth
century B.C. till the nineteenth A.D. and the Romantic
Revival, this "lonely-hearted crag" remained mostly
lost in cloud. For the Classic Fontenelle Aeschylus is
"une espèce de fou"; for the Classic Dryden he "tears
it upon the tripos". He was, indeed, "huge as a mountain, and they hated him".

In Euripides, the rival who superseded him in later
antiquity and criticizes him in his own plays as well as
in the *Frogs* of Aristophanes, there appears Romance of
another type. It was for uncontrolled imagination that
strict Classicism attacked Homer and Aeschylus; it is
for the other Romantic fault, uncontrolled passion, that
Euripides was above all condemned. They had sinned
against the reality-principle; he outrages the super-ego
of his contemporaries. Eros is indeed the most Romantic
of the Immortals, more even than Dionysus; for passion
is a headier intoxicant even than wine. "Speaking in
a perpetual hyperbole", runs the dry phrase of Bacon,
"is comely in nothing but love." Aeschylus, lover of
hyperbole as he was, boasts in the *Frogs* of never having
staged woman in that state (though it would be unfair
to forget the strange wild passion between his Achilles
and Patroclus which still quivers in the fragments of his
lost *Myrmidons*); but a new note rings out in the lines of
Euripides' lost *Stheneboea*:

Love turns to a poet
Even the heart that was sealed to song before.[1]

---

[1] Cf. the adorable lines on Lord Falkland's grandfather in Burford
Church, composed by the dead man's wife:

Love made me poet,
And this I writt,
My harte did doe yt,
And not my witt.

Here stands one of the simple truths that Classicism too often forgot.

Familiar is Lucian's story of the Romantic Revival in Abdera, city renowned for its human geese, when the performance by a strolling company of the *Andromeda* of Euripides sent the whole place mad, so that the streets were filled with pale-faced gentlemen declaiming—

O Love, high sovran lord of Gods and men!

We who possess *Romeo and Juliet* and *Antony and Cleopatra* cannot share the rage of Aristophanes at this first staging of romantic passion; any more than, remembering Macbeth's Porter, we can sympathize much when the rags in which Euripides loved to disguise his characters become red rags to the comic poet. It is merely interesting to note how already Romanticism joins hands with Realism, as the dramatist turns for new subjects to slaves, barbarians, and women, whom the city of Athena treated as inferior beings. Only here again the search for new sensations led the poet down stranger paths, to the incest of Phaedra and of Canace.

But the colours of Romance lie most clearly of all on the mountains of *The Bacchae*, lit by the last rays of the old poet's genius. Among the many-sided meanings of that mystery-play it is not altogether fanciful to find there an allegory of Romanticism itself; to see in the puritanic and pedantic Pentheus a dim ancestor of "one Boileau"; to hear the chants of the Maenads shrilling down the centuries to reverberate on the first night of *Hernani*.

All the mountain there
Went wild and revelled with them—all its beasts—
And all the waste was quickened, leapt and lived.

Euripides reserves his own judgement in this eternal conflict between the forces of self-expression and of self-control; he has not recanted; he is still a Greek and a questioner. But it is as if this tired thinker in his last exile among the wilds of Macedonia, where in real life queens could still dance braceleted with writhing serpents, had felt like many another the call of Nature's tameless energy and the ecstasy, unsicklied by self-questioning, of that Noble Savage, who has since danced like a will-o'-the-wisp before the vision of Rousseau, of Chateaubriand, of D. H. Lawrence. For indeed Dionysus is god as well as beast and no mere phantom of a Romantic dream. "Exuberance is beauty"—"Energy is Eternal Delight"—"Those who restrain desire do so because theirs is weak enough to be restrained". So rings his gospel through the mouth of his prophet Blake. It is an Everlasting Gospel: though it is not the only one.

But the day of Greece was ending; as its sun descended, there spread eastward the giant shadow of Rome. The time of great deeds was over; in that after-twilight, Romance, bird of the dusk, re-opens its dreamy wings. The future was dark; the present drab; men turned perforce to the past. The fourth century B.C., like the eighteenth A.D., had been an age of prose, of oratory, of philosophy; as in France after Napoleon, so here after Alexander, there came a new wave of Romantic poetry. In the dusty streets of his great city, Alexandria, poets dreamed of young shepherds piping, as in the Golden Age, by the blue sea of Sicily; in its dusty libraries they dreamed of young adventurers in the morning of the world steering, beyond the blue Symplegades, out into unknown seas to win the love of passionate witch-maidens in whispering palaces of the East. The countryside of Theocritus looks forward to the countryside of Wordsworth

and Tennyson; the Medea of Apollonius Rhodius to the
Dido of Virgil, the Medea of Ovid, and all those Legends
of Fair Women that haunted mediaeval Romance.

But Rome entered on the heritage of Alexander. The
legions mounted the Acropolis. The precious vase of the
Greek city-state fell shattered, the fragrance of its
Hellenism flowing away down the channels of a grey
cosmopolitanism. The poet found himself no longer a
citizen, but a lonely human soul, face to face with the
impersonal vastness of humanity. All the more he turned
back to the romance of individual passion, like Meleager
the Gadarene with his Heliodora and his Zenophil; or
to the romance of Nature's changing, yet changeless
beauty, which his active forefathers had not dallied to
dream over; or to the romance of laments far lovelier
than Ossian's over the ruined glories of the past. Still
Pan lived on; still, as in Greece to-day,

> High up the mountain-meadows, Echo with never a
> tongue
> Sings back to each bird in answer the song each bird
> hath sung.

Still the sea-birds called, where once the city stood.

> Where are the towers that crowned thee, high-throned
> between thy waters?
> Thy beauty, Dorian Corinth, thy fame of ancient days?
> Thy temples of the Blessed, thy palaces, thy daughters
> Far-sprung from ancient Sisyphus, thy myriad-trodden
> ways?
> Not a trace, not a trace, unhappy, hast thou left behind
> in falling—
> All has been seized and ravened by the wild throat
> of war:
> We only, Ocean's children, still hover calling, calling,
> The sea-mews of thy sorrows, along thy lonely shore.

And now the last child of the Greek genius was born, of partly oriental parentage—the prose-romance, which was to influence those romances of the sixteenth and seventeenth centuries, which have in their turn bequeathed us the word "romantic". These Greek productions of the second and third centuries of the Empire are romantic indeed; dream-dramas of an imagination that takes refuge from reality in a vague world with little historical colouring to date it. Their general character is best summarized in Johnson's epitome of the romantic drama of his own day—so little does the essential recipe of popular "romance" vary through the centuries: "To bring a lover, a lady, and a rival into the fable; to entangle them in contradictory obligations, perplex them with oppositions of interest, and harass them with violence of desires inconsistent with each other; to make them meet in rapture and part in agony; to fill their mouths with hyperbolical joy and outrageous sorrow; to distress them as nothing human ever was distressed; to deliver them as nothing human ever was delivered." To-day no one reads them, hardly—let alone learns them by heart like the young Racine in his boyish defiance of the Puritanism of Port-Royal; but we still remember the Hero and Leander of Musaeus, whose verse romance is almost the farewell of Greek poetry.

There is much, then, that is "Romantic" in classical Greek literature: yet it would be easy to exaggerate. Homer is never unreal as Spenser is; Aeschylus never outrages common sense or common taste like Marlowe. Previous to the Greek novels of the decadence, the Greek dithyramb seems to have gone deepest in intoxication; and was rewarded with the proverbial phrase "silly as a dithyramb". Perhaps that is why hardly any of them have survived. But, in general, the lasting triumph of Greek literature seems to me largely due to its restraint in this as in other things—its balance between Classicism, Realism, and Romanticism, sense and sensibility, fact and fantasy, dryness and ecstasy.

Rome is on the whole more Classical. Characteristic is Livy's definition of a Roman gentleman—"haud minus libertatis alienae quam suae dignitatis memor". Livy does not say: "dignitatis alienae...suae libertatis." For a man's self, dignity comes before freedom. And yet, there is a touch of the Romantic spirit also in this historian who turns, like Malory, from the corruption of his own day to the knightly virtues of a simpler past; and falls too much in love with that picture to be always faithful to fact. Tacitus, again, can be Romantic like Michelet, as his vision flits from province to province of the Empire at whose gate the barbarians are already hammering with the Middle Ages in their train; or idealizes, with a touch of Rousseau, the noble savagery of Germany. There is Romance in Ovid with his love-lorn heroines and his tales of wonder, though Ovid is really too sly and wakeful a wit to lapse into the true Romantic dream; in Virgil, with his Messianic broodings and his passionate Dido; in Catullus, the Roman Burns; in Propertius, the Roman Rossetti, whose cloudy colours are so far, already, from the sharp flame-tongues of Sappho. It is very typical, this difference between the Greek poetess and the two Romans. Sappho may write with "heart of madness"; but her hand does not shake, her tongue falter, nor her vision lose its clarity, even when she details with the nakedness of a medical dictionary, yet the grace

of a perfect utterance, the symptoms of physical passion—
its stammering and quivering and hammering in her
ears. In the days when his own love was still young,
happy and unspoiled, Catullus translated this poem by
the poetess of Lesbos for his "Lesbia"; then, when the
time of rancour and disillusion followed, he wrote
another poem of parting malediction in the same metre,
but this time with words of his own. And now at once
we are in a more Romantic world. His wounded imagination breaks away to wander through the wide provinces
of the Empire, from far Arabia to

> The Gallic Rhine and Britain, Isle of Dread
> And Last of Lands.

Here, and in the brutal realism of his farewell curse,
or the sob of his last likening of his love to a flower
uprooted, like Burns's daisy, by the plough, we seem to
have already travelled half-way from the clear peaks
of the Aegean to the Romantic mists of Ayr. Sappho
too, indeed, speaks in a fragment of the purple hyacinth
that the shepherds' feet trample unregarding on the
hills: but that is in a chorus where young men are
picturing the wasted life of the maid unwed. It was
Catullus who transferred the flower to his own wasted
love with a self-pity that I suspect Sappho's pride would
have refused. In the same way the flawless marble relief
of her vision of Aphrodite remains far removed from the
sombre Rembrandtesque shadows of that night-piece,
Cynthia's Ghost, by Propertius, whose gloom recalls the
race that has filled its tombs in Tuscany with frescoed
nightmares nearer to Udolpho than to Athens.

More Romantic still is the picaresque novel of the
African Apuleius under the Antonines—that strange

figure who lectured on Plato, yet believed in magic and was himself impeached for having bewitched his own wife to marry him. The story of Cupid and Psyche told in his *Golden Ass*[1] by an old hag in a robbers' den looks back to the fairy folklore of Cinderella and forward to the mediaeval allegory, to the idealism of the *Vita Nuova*, to the charm of *Aucassin and Nicolette*, to the *Odes* of Keats, to the *Earthly Paradise* of Morris. Here Apuleius ventures further out of the realm of real life into fabulous fantasy than Homer had ever dared. Not only can his animals talk, like the horse of Achilles; even a tower recites most serviceable instructions for travel in the Netherworld. Aeolus had shut the winds in a bag; on the analogy of bellows, that was quite imaginable; but here, far more mysteriously, Proserpine breathes her own Beauty into a box for Psyche, the soul—and when the box is opened that Beauty is the sleep of Death. And yet, lovely as the story is, with the Classical sense of reality has faded also the Classical grasp of character.

But these things remain only half-Romantic—still self-possessed rather than possessed—compared with what seems to me really the first chant, the prologue, of the Middle Ages—that *Pervigilium Veneris*, *The Vigil of Venus*, probably of the fourth century A.D., which Walter Pater has interwoven with his own romance of *Marius the Epicurean*.

> Cras amet qui nunquam amavit, quique amavit cras amet:
> Ver novum, ver iam canorum, ver renatus orbis est;
> Vere concordant amores, vere nubunt alites,
> Et nemus comam resolvit de maritis imbribus.
> Cras amet qui nunquam amavit, quique amavit cras amet.

[1] It is significant that Charles Nodier, the French Romantic, had a boundless admiration for the book and imitated it.

Cras amorum copulatrix inter umbras arborum
Implicat casas virentes de flagello myrteo;
Cras canoris feriatos ducit in silvis choros;
Cras Dione iura dicit fulta sublimi throno.
Cras amet qui nunquam amavit, quique amavit cras amet.

Loveless hearts shall love to-morrow, hearts that have
  loved shall love again.
Spring is young, and spring is singing, spring is life where
  death had lain.
Spring is time of true love's knitting, in the spring the
  birds are wed,
Under the rain of her lord's blessing the forest waves her
  leafy head.
Loveless hearts shall love to-morrow, hearts that have
  loved shall love again.

In the shadow of the woodland she that binds all true
  hearts' vows,
She shall build them bowers to-morrow of her own green
  myrtle boughs;
Yea, to-morrow shall Diōne dance them down the
  greenwood shaw
And Love's Lady high-enthronèd on her lovers lay her law.
Loveless hearts shall love to-morrow, hearts that have
  loved shall love once more.

Here in this pagan *Song of Songs* is already the mediaeval
passion for passion, with the lilt of the mediaeval lyric.
Already the birds are making ready for St Valentine.
Botticelli himself never painted a lovelier Spring, nor
a lovelier Venus; and yet the same wistful sorrow haunts
this spring-song of the old world's autumn as over-
shadows the dreamy faces on his canvases. For Pan is
dying. Behind the desperate passion of these leaping
trochees, wilder than anything in Latin before them
except the Oriental *Atys* of Catullus, thuds the tramp of
the barbarians along the roads to Rome, where men

are turning away from the full-flushed Mother of Eros to the Virgin Mother of Christ.

This poem, indeed, rises like a watershed between two worlds. Behind falls the long straight Roman Way; in front stretch the cloudy valleys of the Middle Ages with, far off, the winding lanes of the Wandering Scholars and the meadows of England where the cuckoo sings for summer and "Lenten ys come with Love to toune". Here already we can catch an echo of the distant melodies of Benedictbeuern, eight hundred years away.

> Estivant nunc Dryades
> Colle sub umbroso.
> Prodeunt Oreades
> Coetu glorioso.
> Satyrorum concio
> Psallit cum tripudio
> Tempe per amena:
> His alludens concinit,
> Cum iucundi meminit
> Veris, filomena.

> Down the woods the Dryades
>   Wander now a-maying:
> Now the proud Oreiades
>   High on hills are straying.
> Through the happy valleys green
> Harping, singing, now is seen
>   Many a goatish dancer:
> While in gladness for the spring
> Philomena carolling
>   Makes them merry answer.

Why is it that the Middle Ages have seemed so long the native soil of Romance, the Well at the World's End where it rises, the Wood beyond the World where it runs wild? There have already been many touches

of Romance in the Classics; yet these keep some sense
of incongruity about them. They surprise, like strange
plants sown by some wandering bird or wind in fields
far from their home; such as that Druid mistletoe, to
which Virgil compares his Golden Bough, the mystic
passport to another world than ours:

> Quale solet silvis brumai frigore viscum
> Fronde virere nova, quod non sua seminat arbos
> Et croceo fetu teretis circumdare truncos.

> As in December's frost the mistletoe
> Puts forth new shoots upon an alien tree,
> Wreathing with saffron fruit its columned bole.

So Romance blooms only sparsely here and there in
the oak-groves of Antiquity; but in the Middle Ages
it is everywhere, like the mistletoe in orchards of Nor-
mandy. Romance is young. "You Greeks are ever
children", said the Egyptian priest; but the Middle
Ages are more childlike still. Romance is an uncritical
love of wonders; and the Middle Ages believed nearly
everything they heard and everything they read. All
books were Gospel-true; it was long yet to the day when
Francis Bacon was to set the fashion of regularly testing
theory by experiment. He died of the cold he caught
stuffing a fowl with snow; of that new attitude our
modern world was born. But the mediaeval mind is
content to read in Pliny that the traveller who takes
a myrtle-staff will never feel tired—how interesting!—
copy it out. Test it?—why? Pliny's word is good enough.
Albertus Magnus says a woman will confess all her
secrets, if a frog's tongue is laid on her heart as she sleeps;
but few men stirred out to catch a frog. Doubt was only
possible if the authority was *not* sufficiently antique.

Topsell judiciously suspends judgement on the power of virgins to ensnare unicorns, because he can find "no *elder* authority than Tzetzes, who did not live *above* five hundred years ago". No wonder, then, they could believe anything. The Abbot Richalm of Schöntal in the fourteenth century warns us that even flea-bites are not flea-bites—they are really the work of devils. Edward II can write to the Pope asking if without sin he may use an ointment that gives courage (he was to need it, poor soul). And Hubert de Burgh can be solemnly accused of having abstracted from the royal treasury a ring that made the wearer invincible, and sent it to Llewelyn. It is a happy touch in *The Cloister and the Hearth* when a character, asked the meaning of a crowd in the street, replies: "Ye born fool! it's only a miracle!". Similarly, Luther, wakened by a noise in the night, turns over and goes to sleep again—it is *only* the Devil.

It is interesting to find even a mediaeval writer drawing the line occasionally, like the author of *Ider*[1]—

> Tels diz n'a fors savor de songe,
> Tant en acreissent les paroles;
> Mes jo n'ai cure d'iperboles:
> Yperbole est chose non voire,
> Qui ne fu et n'est a croire,
> C'en est la difinicion:
> Mes tant di de cest paveillon
> Qu'il n'en a nul soz ciel qu'il vaille.

"There are some stories like dreams, so exaggerated are they; but I have no use for hyperboles. 'Hyperbole' is a thing that never was, and is past belief—that is its definition. But I *will* say for this pavilion I am de-

[1] Quoted by W. P. Ker, *Epic and Romance* (1897), p. 379.

scribing, that there is not its like under the sun." But the builders of Seville Cathedral had no such fear of "hyperbole": "It shall be so great", they resolved, "that posterity shall think us mad." There speaks true Romance.

No doubt Greece and Rome had their superstitions. An eclipse of the moon nearly ruined Greece in the Persian War, and did ruin Athens before Syracuse. Plato, again, tells us a legend of an invisible ring. But Plato puts it on the finger of a legendary Oriental in a tale avowedly mythical. We cannot conceive Cleon asking Delphi if he would be tortured in Hades for fortifying his poor nerves with magic ointment. A Universe where even fleas are devils is less comfortable than ours; but this anarchy of unseen wills was far more dramatically personal than our mechanic conception of the scientific uniformity behind all the world's variety, of the few simple laws behind all its transformations. For mediaeval man, always anything might happen. We still talk of the wonders of Nature; but Nature has become like a mass of stage machinery, with not a soul on the boards. "I beseech you, my brethren," once cried a Bampton lecturer, "by the mercies of Christ, that you hold fast the integrity of your anthropomorphism." The Greek with nymph and faun, the mediaeval mind with fay and goblin, had sources of imaginative excitement that have since run dry. There may be substitutes; but it is cant to pretend that Science has not left life less dramatic. The ring of Saturn is not the ring of Venus.

This abeyance of the critical faculty, of the sense of reality, seems, then, one source of the romance of the Middle Ages. It left men's imaginations vague, vast, and free. They believed what they read, and what they believed, they embroidered. But what did they read? Some of the classics; but also more unrestrained works such as the Bible and the lives of the Saints (followed later by the influence of Arabia). So that now Jordan flowed into Tiber, with all the Eastern imagination and imagery of the Old Testament, the miracles of Moses, the ecstasies of the *Song of Solomon*. "Thy neck is as a tower of ivory; thine eyes like the fishpools in Heshbon by the gate of Bath-rabbim; thy nose is as the tower of Lebanon that looketh towards Damascus." "Longinus" had admired the noble bareness of *Genesis*—"God said, Let there be light: and there was light"; but how he would have shuddered at this cascade of similes, such as even Aeschylus never dreamt of! The Bible has contributed its share, not merely by stories like those of Rachel, Ruth, and Esther, but by its whole style and atmosphere, to European Romantic literature. For the very same reason it was typical that in the age of neo-Classicism the Maréchale de Luxembourg should lament, opening the sacred text, that the Holy Spirit should have had "si peu de goût", or that Voltaire should be content to render those other words of the *Song of Solomon*: "His eyes are as the eyes of doves by the rivers of waters, washed with milk, and fitly set" by the bald "Un feu pur est dans ses yeux".[1] Here lies in little the whole

[1] An English eighteenth-century poet can treat the Bible less baldly but worse: in the hands of Francis Fawkes (1761), Jaël's "butter in a lordly dish" (symbol of the simple milk of human kindness and of the deference of hospitality in grim contrast with the treachery behind) becomes—

> He ask'd refreshment from the limpid wave:
> The milky beverage to the chief she gave.

How rancid it has turned!

difference between the Romantic and the neo-Classic spirit—the refusal of the second to dream. "Je vais droit au fait—c'est ma devise", said Voltaire; it was his motto in poetry also. "Un feu pur est dans ses yeux"—they are eyes to discern with, but not to gaze in.

Further, if the Middle Ages were made even more imaginative by what they read, they also made what they read more imaginative. Their translations are new creations. Their wondering child-like naïveté transforms everything they touch; as when Caxton with reckless inaccuracy—how be accurate in a dream?—sets his hand to Ovid. Here he is the exact reverse of Voltaire with the *Song of Songs*. The easy insolent ease of the frivolous courtier of Augustus is now replaced by the struggling accents of a child construing; and yet what new seriousness, what new wonder and mystery gather round us, as Caxton tiptoes, for example, into that favourite resort of Romantic dreamers, the House of Sleep!—"The hows of this gode was in a most still place of the worlde in the bottom of the kreves of a mountayne, where as the sonne never shyneth, where as it seemeth aleway is betwyn day and nyght. There slepeth this god. Ther is neyther noyse ne lyghte may dystrowble hys reste. There resowneth nothynge but a swete wynd amonge rosyers. And a lytil broke of water soundeth, whych renneth and murmureth upon the gravell that it resowneth forto gyve appetyte to sleep."

The glamour does not lie merely in the quaint spelling; and yet even this adds to it—not simply by being old. A whole psychological difference has developed between us whose careful proof-readers are up in arms if we spell the same word differently a hundred pages apart, and these half-conscious forefathers of ours who did not centre their minds on such trivialities, quite content, even as late as Elizabeth, to spell Sir Thomas More's surname three ways in one line. Is our anxious alertness wholly gain? It would have seemed slavish pedantry to men that could rebel even against the laws of grammar; like the Emperor Sigismund, who pronounced that a Holy Roman Emperor was above it; or Pope Gregory the Great who wrote: "Casus servare contemno quia indignum vehementer esistimo ut verba coelistis oraculi restringam sub regulis Donati".

But the Parnassus of mediaeval romance, like that of the Romantic Revival, has twin summits. If this freedom of fantasy is one, freedom of passion is the other. Here too a verse of the *Song of Songs* will serve for text. "Many waters cannot quench love, neither can the floods drown it; if a man would give all the substance of his house for love, it would utterly be contemned." Set beside this the sober wisdom of Homer:

Of all things cometh surfeit, even of love and sleep,
Of sweet song and of dances that faultless measure keep.

For Homer, Passion is not life's crown; only one bright ring on its fair finger, where shine others no less bright. Not that he belittles the wedding-ring. It is enough to remember Andromache, and Penelope, and Odysseus' praise of marriage to Nausicaa in her queenly girlhood, as he blesses her at their first meeting. Nor does Homer despise physical passion—it too is the gift of a goddess, lovely and terrible. Troy is destroyed for one woman, the Greek host nearly ruined for another, and Ithaca for

a third. All the same, for Homeric wisdom Love is not
a matter for mystic rhapsodies. Nothing is. The later
ages of Pericles and Demosthenes were still less in love
with love. Plato believed in woman's education; but
not in chivalry. "The characters in tragedy", remarks
Aristotle in his cold, even voice, "should be good. Even
a woman, or a slave, *may* be good." We are not far here
from the Orient and the seraglio.

Things were otherwise with the women of the Feudal
Age, who could even inherit fiefs themselves; a system
that helped to cost the Franks their hold on mediaeval
Greece. On the other hand women, if sisters to the
Virgin, were daughters of Eve and vessels of sin. And
yet even this sense of guilt helped still more to dramatize
passion. To the pagan, love the "bitter-sweet" might
bring heart-ache, rarely heart-break; but for the
Christian it might mean a soul writhing in everlasting
flame. "Why is the sun red at sunset?" "Because he
goeth towards Hell." Two of the most dramatic figures
of the mediaeval imagination largely owe their intensity
to this lurid light from the Christian underworld—
Faust[1] and Don Juan. Against that red background
loved Abelard and Héloise, Henry Plantagenet and
Rosamund Clifford, Paolo and Francesca, Tristram and
Iseult, Lancelot and Guenevere. When Alexander came
to Anchialus, he read on the statue of the Assyrian
king: "Sardanapalus built Anchialus and Tarsus on the

[1] How many know that imaginative touch in the old Faust-legend,
unused by Marlowe or Goethe, which tells how that doomed body, as
it lay on its bier, turned of itself face downwards from the wrath of God?
Five times it was laid on its back; five times it was found with its forehead
to the earth; and so left at last. (J. Gast, *Convivialium Sermonum Liber* II,
1544.) Such a fantasy of terror is hardly to be found in all paganism.

same day; but thou, stranger, eat, drink and make love; all else is not worth—that!" To the Greek this was always a possible view even if, like Alexander, he did not follow its Epicureanism. But when Tannhäuser turned to the hollow mountain of pagan love, it seemed a sin too terrible for Rome itself to absolve.

Heaven, too, added its force, as well as Hell, to this idealizing of passion. Beside Francesca stands Beatrice. For the muddled mediaeval mind could never really decide whether passion were sin or salvation. "While she lived, she was a true lover," writes Malory of Guenevere, "and *therefore* she had a good end." It was not to her husband she was true; but no matter—like the Magdalene, *multum amavit*. Malory did not think it out; he likewise had loved her too well.

Here, then, in the Middle Ages we have reached a new stage in the growth of Romanticism. It is no longer simply the passionate or fantastic dreaming of a roving imagination that has shaken off the too insistent claims of Society or Reality. Society itself has now grown Romantic; it has built up a new creed and a new code of conduct. "True lovers come to good ends." Such a faith is a foreshadowing of the beliefs about the sanctity of all passion, the divine origin of all love, that were to lead to such extravagances in the days of Rousseau and George Sand. The madness of the imagination has now begun to acquire a method; the blind pagan Cupid to found an established Church. *L'amour courtois* develops an elaborate convention; its very first article is that it cannot exist between wife and husband, only between wife and lover. Again, under the more familiar shape of chivalry, mediaeval romance has bequeathed to us standards of action not yet wholly dead. From the race of knights-errant, crossed with the brigand, the noble savage, and the rebellious Satan, the pedigree of Romantic heroes descends, through the fairy-world of Tasso and Spenser and the over-heroic stage of Dryden, to the gloomy supermen or misanthropes of Byron and Monk Lewis, Anne Radcliffe and Emily Brontë.

There is no more charming incarnation of these mediaeval ideas than Aucassin; and there could hardly be a clearer contrast than his story offers with the Greek world, even at its most Romantic. Like Achilles, Aucassin refuses to fight because the woman he loves is taken away. But Homer hardly tells us how Briseis looked, or how Achilles felt for her. 'She remains in his hands a dazzling shadow—"fair-cheeked", "like golden Aphrodite"; it was mediaeval Romance that first woke her to real life, two thousand years later, under the too famous name of Cressida. Even the beauty of Helen herself is never described by the Greek poet. How vividly, by contrast, Nicolette looks out of her prison-window in Beaucaire, or clambers down from it by her rope of sheets and towels! "She had fair hair with little curls, and her eyes blue-grey and laughing, and her face well-featured, and her nose high and well set, and her lips redder than cherry or rose in summertide, and her teeth white and little; and her breasts were hard, lifting her robe as if they had been two walnuts; and so slim she was from flank to flank that you might have clasped her within your two hands; and the daisy-flowers broken by her toes, as they fell across the arch of her foot, were right black against her feet and legs—so white was the maid." This Nicolette is the very ecstasy of a lover's dream.

Homer, again, never leaves Achilles heart-broken for his Briseis. Pride and anger are his ruling passions, not love; and Patroclus meant more to him than a hundred women. So with Menelaus and Helen. Round her the whole war is fought; but again it is a point of honour more than love. Whereas Aucassin is wholly besotted with the thought of Nicolette, whom his father has refused him. For one promised kiss he finally consents to take the field. But he is still lost in dreams of her, as he rides into the battle; he is taken prisoner and led off to death; only then does he suddenly awake and hew his captors down. Homer's audience would have thought this an excessively moon-struck young man.

"What use", says Hector to himself, as he sees Achilles advancing like death across the Trojan plain, "what use for me to speak with him?—not for us such love-talk as the whispers of youth and maid!" This one fleeting, bitter glimpse of young romance Homer gives us, like a last ray of sunlight before darkness closes on the plain of Troy; but he never brings youth and maid to whisper their love before us, like the author of *Aucassin*:

"Yet I would rather die, than know you had lain in another man's bed than mine."

"Ai," said she, "I do not believe you love me so much as you say: but I love you better than you love me."

"Nay," said Aucassin, "fair, sweet friend! It may not be that you should love me as I you. Women cannot love man as man loves woman. For woman's love is in her eye, and the tip of her breast, and the tip of her toe; but man's love is planted in his heart within, and cannot out."

Charming, foolish metaphysics—part meaningless, part untrue—the perfect fantasy of lovers. It is as prettily unreal as the instant healing of Aucassin's dislocated shoulder by the white fingers of Nicolette—"for so God willed, who loveth lovers". "All the world", the saying still goes, "loves a lover"; certainly this mediaeval world did so; and remade even its God in its own image.

And yet, elsewhere in this romance, there appears a very different theology: "'If you made her your paramour...all the days of Eternity your soul would lie in Hell—into Paradise you would come never.' 'In Paradise what have I to do? I care not to come there, if I can have Nicolette, my sweet friend that I love so.'" There is no need to quote the rest—the most famous passage in the whole story—with its vision of old priests and cripples and beggars hobbling heavenward, while the good knights and the ladies with their lovers two or three, the minstrels and the poets, the gold and silver sweep gaily down to hell. For a moment Aucassin stands there defiant on the mountain-top, with Satan, with Prometheus, and with Manfred. So native is rebellion to Romance. God and Mother Church provide a father-substitute, a super-ego, to rebel against. Homer's Odysseus too passes the gate of Hell; but in sorrowful obedience, not in defiance. Greek wisdom knew too well that, however brave our words, it is vain work for mortals to battle with the gods.

Again, the mediaeval artist, more childish, shows far less feeling than the Greek for unity of tone. There is, indeed, enough comic relief in Homer to shock the neo-Classics badly—things like the burlesque life on Olympus, or Irus the beggar, or Ajax slipping into the offal. But there is never anything fantastic enough to endanger the seriousness of the whole; whereas when Aucassin comes to the land of Torelore (enchanting name), we

seem suddenly translated from Spenser to Rabelais or
Lewis Carroll, from the *Iliad* to the *Battle of Frogs and
Mice*. Torelore is at war, its queen at the front, its king
in bed. Why? Because the queen has just had a child.
Aucassin, outraged, cudgels the monarch out of bed;
together they ride to the war and find a battle raging,
the air darkened with a barrage of eggs and roast crab-
apples, fresh cheeses and giant mushrooms. Aucassin
at once starts hewing the enemy down; but the king
cries "Hold!" It is not at all the custom of Torelore
that in battles people should be killed!

In Homer, again, the realism of his humbler folk is
never in danger of making ridiculous the heroic side of
his story. Thersites[1] is speedily silenced; the swineherd
of Odysseus remains "the god-like swineherd", himself
a king's son. But in *Aucassin* there suddenly appears
a grotesque peasant figure with the Sancho-Panzan
common sense of a Shakespearean fool. "He had a great
shock-head, blacker than coal, and more than a palm's
breadth between his eyes; great cheeks and a huge flat
nose and great gaping nostrils and blubber-lips redder
than a beef-steak and great ugly yellow teeth." He asks
Aucassin why he is weeping. "For a fair white grey-
hound" he has lost, is Aucassin's symbolic reply. "Listen
to him!" exclaims the outraged peasant, "crying for
a stinking hound! Foul befall him who ever respects
you again!" The poor villein has himself lost an ox
and in his destitution his old mother has had the very
mattress dragged from under her. Here is something
real to cry for. "Love does not vex the man that begs

---

[1] And even Thersites was too realistically low for the Renaissance
critic Vida (*Poetica*, II, 179–90).

his bread"—Euripides, too, had said it. But no Athenian ever embodied that truth in so grotesque, yet vivid a shape as this. And yet the romance survives this proletarian realism; the love of Nicolette does not become absurd; just as Rosalind is not extinguished by Touchstone. The Greeks staged a burlesque after each tragic trilogy: but they did not mix things with this Romantic insouciance of the mediaeval mind.

If Aucassin is the perfect lover of Romance, Lancelot is its perfect knight. This sterner ideal rings out immortally in that lament of Sir Ector over Lancelot, which recalls, far off, the lamentations in Homer over Hector dead: "Ah Launcelot," he said, "thou were head of all Christian knights, and now I dare say, said Sir Ector, thou Sir Launcelot, there thou liest, that thou were never matched of earthly knight's hand. And thou were the courteoust knight that ever bare shield. And thou were the truest friend to thy lover that ever bestrad horse. And thou were the truest lover of a sinful man that ever loved woman. And thou were the kindest man that ever struck with sword. And thou were the goodliest person that ever came among press of knights. And thou was the meekest man and the gentlest that ever ate in hall among ladies. And thou were the sternest knight to thy mortal foe that ever put spear in the rest."

Here Romantic chivalry cries its last challenge in the face of death: the human spirit has framed few prouder endings. Though there is perhaps more of the essence of Romance in sentences elsewhere in Malory, such as "Then, as they rode, they heard by them a great horse grimly neigh and then were they ware of a knight that lay all armed under an apple-tree"; or "'Fair fellow,' said Sir Ector, 'knowest thou in this country any adventures that be here nigh hand?'" If only he could always have written so! But, like most of his age, Malory lacks sense of form. He sometimes grows muddled in his story-telling, as in his ideas; so that it remains hard, I think, to understand how T. E. Lawrence could take the *Morte d'Arthur* as his companion in the wastes of Arabia; and pronounce, after translating the *Odyssey*, that it was a creeping poem after all. The *Odyssey* seems to me, on the contrary, a standing proof of the superiority of work that, with all its Romantic dreaming, yet maintains to the end Classic sanity and self-control.

But the *Morte d'Arthur* is the testament of a dying age. Like his Sir Bedivere, Malory is left sighing in his solitude for a world of chivalry that has already passed away: a fifteenth-century Don Quixote, watching indignantly while round him the Pastons and their like are laying the new foundations of an England of shopkeepers; a stone crusader, stark in his armour on his grey tomb, amid the grosser, more vital figures of Breughel's world. For now above the ashes of the fair dames of yesteryear, of Elaine and Iseult and Ettarre, François Villon is already chanting, with a leer at all Romance:

> Folles amours font les gens bestes:
> Salmon en ydolatria,
> Samson en perdit ses lunettes.
> Bien est eureux qui riens n'y a.

> Follies of love leave an addled pate,
> Love bowed to idols Solomon's wit,
> Samson, he lost his eyes that gate,
> Lucky are they that are quit of it.

And in the dust gathering on Malory's monument Ascham was soon to scrawl that characteristic libel of Renaissance hatred for the Middle Ages—that the painter of Lancelot and Galahad cared only for "open manslaughter and bold bawdry". For a moment the pedant of the Reformation seems to echo the poet of Catholicism: "Galeotto fu il libro, e chi lo scrisse".

Sometimes, it is true, the Renaissance tried to combine the old Romance with the new Classics. With Ronsard and Shakespeare it triumphed. With others the attempt was less happy. The Romantic elements in ancient literature had been, in the main, either dreams of far fairylands and pastoral Arcadias or else the heart's cry of natural passion. But these Renaissance attempts show the self-consciousness that besets all literary revivals: and as the essence of Romanticism is that it should draw freely on the fantasies that rise from half-conscious dreaming, any self-conscious bookishness proves particularly deadly to it. This wild hyacinth withers in a *parterre* or a vase. Already in antiquity, when Apollonius Rhodius or Propertius become antiquarians, they become bores; it is their scenes of passion alone that live. In Tasso, or Spenser, or Sidney's *Arcadia* there is a sickly taint of the factitious, of pastiche. These writers fall between two worlds, between two periods. Spenser is a witching painter, in the style of Claude Lorraine; but he can neither tell a tale nor create a character. Even Ariosto, who shields himself behind a mocker's grin, with his interminable necromancers and magic steeds gives too much the impression of a grown man in a green garden playing at bears. And even in Shakespeare's *Tempest* Prospero's wand, I feel, has already cracked a little before he flings it from him; his magic volume grown a little dog-eared, before he closes it for ever. Prospero is too close a cousin to Polonius, without seeming aware of the relationship; and his daughter remains a pretty poppet, beginning to fade into a Spenserian decline. In Beaumont and Fletcher this malady of unreality has gone further; in the prose romances of the seventeenth century it grows incurable; the Heroic Drama of the Restoration is its raucous death-rattle. How was it still possible after *Don Quixote* to write *Don Sebastian*!

The ancient world had been, at its height, acutely self-critical. "Know Thyself"—"Nothing Too Much" —so spoke the temple at its central Delphi. Apollo's priestess might rave; but not Apollo. Even the raving priestess raved in hexameters. The Middle Ages had swung away into uncritical credulity. Now with neo-Classicism self-consciousness returns. But it returns in excess. "Metaphysical poetry" is an extraordinary example of leaping from one extreme to its opposite— from honey to cayenne pepper. Men had grown weary of Spenser beautifully dreaming in his House of Sleep, in the bed where Ovid and Caxton had already lain—

> Here Sleep's House by famous Ariosto,
> By silver-tongued Ovid and many moe—
> Perhaps by golden-mouthed Spenser too, pardie—
> Which builded was some dozen stories high,
> I had repaired, but that it was so rotten
> As Sleep awaked by rats from thence was gotten.[1]

Donne wanted no high-astounding stories; he and his disciples preferred a laboratory on the ground-floor—

[1] Once attributed to Donne; probably by Sir John Roe.

sometimes poisonous, often stuffy, and as somnolent, very often, to the modern visitor as ever the House of Sleep. But these new intellectuals proved, as so often, not very intelligent. For it is as futile, and as fatal, to let the analysing intellect play cat's cradle with the feelings, as to let the feelings besot the intellect. Donne himself has passions strong enough to survive, sometimes, even his own finicking treatment. The cat's cradle bursts into flame. But his followers are mostly caught, like poor flies, in their own tangled cobwebs. "Things divorced in Nature," as old Fuller says in that Metaphysical prose of his, so much more human than most Metaphysical verse, "are married in Fancy as in a lawless place". But, when the divorce in Nature is so violent, Fancy seldom makes a very happy marriage; or a very fruitful one.

The same thing had happened before, in antiquity. After Spenser, Donne; after Sophocles, Lycophron; after Virgil, Seneca. The chamber-tragedies of that provincial Spaniard under the red disillusion of the Empire had likewise been mere verbal bull-fights. His arena is strewn with as many disembowelled hacks as possible—the characters; and the pleasure, apart from simple sadism, consists in watching the infinite deftness with which the poet wields those stabbing darts, that flashing sword, of indefatigable epigram.

But literary toreadors are mostly short-lived. Few things rust faster than the edge of self-conscious cleverness. Marvell's *Coy Mistress*, indeed, will be lovely "till the Conversion of the Jews"; Donne's *Extasie* is ecstatic still; but his *Flea* is little worth hunting, except for those who like to see such things perform. Catullus writes, still Classically clear even in his Romantic frenzy:

> Odi et amo. Quare id faciam, fortasse requiris,
> Nescio. Sed fieri sentio, et excrucior.

> I hate, yet love her. If you ask me why,
> I know not. But 'tis truth; and agony.

But Donne would have pretended to know; and have told us in fifty lines of conceits, mediocre in wit, callous in feeling, and totally indifferent to truth. Cynicism should at least be terse; like La Rochefoucauld or Chamfort. Yet Donne remains a great poet. More typical of his school than its master is Cowley, for a few years one of the world's supreme writers; and then, a few years later—"Who reads Cowley?"

> Pretty in amber to observe the forms
> Of hairs or straws or dirt or grubs or worms!
> The things we know are neither rich nor rare,
> But wonder how the devil they got there.

But those with lives of their own to lead will not waste overlong in wondering. It was, indeed, a European disease of the time. In Italy Marini gave his name to it, and even Dante Alighieri was thought worthy to be praised in puns—

> Ben sull' *ali liggier* tre mondi canta.

The same epidemic raged in France; "la pointe" appeared like a smallpox on the face of everything.

> Un héros sur la scène eut soin de s'en parer,
> Et sans pointe un amant n'osa plus soupirer.

But here too, adds Boileau (alas, too optimistically):

> La raison outragée enfin ouvrit les yeux,
> La chassa pour jamais des discours sérieux.

Mediaeval romance had come to seem literature for children; Metaphysical poetry, apart from a few master-pieces, was an interlude of poetry for coxcombs; it was next replaced by neo-Classic poetry—poetry for gentle-men. You may still be conscious of your wit; but it is bad manners to parade it, and bad sense to waste it on quibbles. And so under Louis XIV and Queen Anne came the great advance of trying to be intelligent rather than clever. It was an honester attitude to reality; a politer attitude to society. But, in a way, it cramped the preconscious side of the mind more tightly than anything before. The Metaphysical brain, as we see it in Fuller or Sir Thomas Browne, had still left loopholes for spontaneous whimsy, fancy, and caprice: the now tightened censorship of the "reality-principle" repressed most of these. The typical eighteenth-century intellectual tried far more to "know himself"; he tried to know himself too much; he failed to guess, even, how much there was he could not know. And in literature he let his society-conscience make a coward of him.

In fact, "gentlemen" have often a narrow taste in things imaginative; sometimes they have none. They seldom wrote as badly as the Metaphysicals; they seldom wrote as well. Poetry came in danger of dying, not indeed of politeness, but of polish. Yet the art of prose, less daemonic, now flourished; so did the art of life. Indeed, if it is asked what is the place in life, as well as letters, of Romance, one cannot do better than contrast the eighteenth century with the age that preceded it and the age that followed. And, as typical, it is worth considering men's change in attitude towards two of the deepest things in life—love and death.

By 1700 the age of Almanzors is over. The plot of *Le Cid*, like that of *Maud*, had turned on the tragic conflict between love and kinship. The hero kills the father, or the brother, of his mistress; the end is nearly death in the one case, is madness in the other. In the eighteenth-century *Gil Blas* this situation of a murdered brother recurs; the lady is still passionately romantic— for we are in Spain; but how coolly realistic is the advice Don Raphaël now gives her distracted lover!—"Il faut oublier cette jeune dame.... Vous trouverez sans doute quelque jeune personne qui fera sur vous la même impression, et dont vous n'aurez pas tué le frère." Le Cid, I feel, finds a deadlier opponent here in Lesage than ever in the father of his Chimène.

"Il faut leur apprendre", says Madame de Maintenon, of young girls, "à aimer raisonnablement, comme à faire toutes choses." Classic utterance! Horace had laughed long since, as the God of Love has always laughed, at such efforts to methodize a madness. And yet Madame de Maintenon was not altogether mad either. Just as swooning and weeping have gone in and out of fashion, so there are ages when the convention is for lovers to be far madder than in others; and the convention is extremely potent. Men may take as their pattern Aeneas leaving Dido for duty, or Titus Bérénice; or they may learn to prefer an Antony and "All for Love; or the World Well Lost". What a contrast, again, between this ideal of "loving reasonably" and the *Lettres d'une Religieuse Portugaise* (1669) with their romantic passion for passion, whatever its misery: "Je suis ravie d'avoir fait tout ce que j'ay fait pour vous contre toute sorte de bienséance: je ne mets plus mon honneur, et ma

religion, qu'à vous aimer éperduement toute ma vie"
—"je vous remercie dans le fond de mon cœur du
désespoir que vous me causez; et je déteste la tranquillité
où j'ay vescu avant que je vous connusse." Here is the
very tone of Byron (it is too often forgotten that he really
was a poet)—or of one side of Byron:

> Their breath is agitation, and their life
> A storm whereon they ride to sink at last,
> And yet so nursed and bigoted to strife,
> That should their days, surviving perils past,
> Melt to calm twilight, they feel overcast
> With sorrow and supineness, and so die;
> Even as a flame unfed that runs to waste
> With its own flickering, or a sword laid by
> Which eats into itself, and rusts ingloriously.

Contrast with these the sad disillusion of Mme de
Staal-Delaunay (1684–1750): "Toute passion s'éteint
dès qu'on voit l'objet tel qu'il est"; or the gay disillusion
of Mme d'Esparbès to the young Lauzun (1747–93):
"Croyez-moi, mon petit cousin, il ne réussit plus d'être
romanesque; cela rend ridicule et voilà tout." So there
grew up in eighteenth-century France a school of
Epicureans, whose motto in love was "Point de lende-
main". Horace Walpole complains that the art of
courtship will soon be reduced to the words, "Lie down".
And even Buffon could write—"Il n'y a de bon dans
l'amour que le physique."

How reason simplifies life! And yet life may refuse
to be simplified. But at least, whatever its over-rational-
ization of love, no age has known better how to die
simply and gracefully than this Age of Reason. The
seventeenth century had faced death with terror, or
bitterness, or the *panache* of Algernon Sidney (1683),

replying to the headsman's question, "Will you rise again? Are you ready, sir?"—"Not till the general Resurrection. Strike on." This is tremendous. And similarly when Romanticism has begun to revive, the emotionalism too returns with Mme Roland's "O Liberté, que de crimes on commet en ton nom!"; or Danton's "Tu montreras ma tête au peuple; elle en vaut la peine!"; or Mirabeau's vanity, as the cannon boomed over Paris—"Sont-ce déjà les funérailles d'Achille?"; or Nelson's "Kiss me, Hardy".

But the society of the eighteenth century had quitted the stage with a lighter touch than this; like Madame de Pompadour, seeing the priest impatient to be gone—"Un moment, monsieur le curé, nous partirons ensemble"; or Mme du Deffand with her ironic "Monsieur le curé, je m'accuse d'avoir contrevenu aux dix commandements de Dieu, et d'avoir commis les sept péchés mortels"; or Chesterfield murmuring, courteous to the end, "Give Dayrolles a chair"; or Adam Smith's calm farewell to his friends—"I believe we must adjourn this meeting to some other place"; or that supreme grace of the Vicomtesse d'Houdetot—"Je me regrette."

Such things, like the music of Handel or Mozart, may make us feel that in some ways, for a small circle, the eighteenth century was the most civilized period there has ever been, with its sense of fact and yet its social grace, its freedom from fanaticism and folly. We owe it more than we know; and we are busy squandering that heritage in the frenzies of this darkening Europe that has so largely exchanged misgovernment by gentlemen for misgovernment by gangsters. There has been written no truer praise of that great period than this passage by J. L. and Barbara Hammond: ''A row of eighteenth-century houses, or a room of normal eighteenth-century furniture, or a characteristic piece of eighteenth-century literature, conveys at once a sense of satisfaction and completeness. The secret of this charm is not to be found in any special beauty or nobility of design or expression, but simply in an exquisite fitness. The eighteenth-century mind was a unity, an order; it was finished and it was simple. All literature and art that really belong to the eighteenth century are the language of a little society of men and women, who moved within one set of ideas; who understood each other; who were not tormented by any anxious or bewildering problems; who lived in comfort and, above all things, in composure. The Classics were their freemasonry.''

But it was not a poetic age, though it has its poetry for us:

> Comme vous meurtrissez les cœurs
> De vos airs charmants et moqueurs
>   Et si tristes,
> Menuets à peine entendus,
> Sanglots légers, rires fondus,
>   Baisers tristes.[1]

> Ah, how heart-rendingly disarming
> Your melodies; so mocking—charming—
>   Yet so *triste*:
> Minuets that whisper sighing,
> Half-heard sobs, low laughs replying,
>   Sad lips kissed.

Even the robust romanticism of Browning felt it, as he listened to a toccata of Galuppi's, while Casanova's Venice, like a ghostly Venus, rose again before him from her sea. No doubt it is dangerously easy to turn romantic

[1] Fernand Gregh.

about the neo-Classic age itself, as the growing distance purples it. But we can well believe, without romancing, the sincerity of that survivor of the old régime who affirmed to a later generation that life before the Revolution had possessed a grace, a charm, nothing could ever give again. It was the privilege of a few, no doubt; but it was real.

Unfortunately men were trying to be more reasonable than it is reasonable to try to be.[1] In life, their ideal was not ignoble: but it was impossible. And in literature, it is not the best ideal for verse that it should be "as fine as prose".[2] Like the boy in the story, who was coated all over with gold paint for a pageant, the human spirit stifled. Poetry tended to grow too like this passage from the *Reflections upon Theatrical Expression*[3] of 1755: "In *Astonishment* and *Surprise* arising from *Terror* the *left leg* is drawn back to some distance from the other: under the same Affection of the Mind, but resulting from an *unhop'd for Meeting* with a beloved Object, the *right leg* is advanced to some distance before the left. *Impatience* and *Regret* at being detected in an iniquitous Design may be heightened by shuffling of the *Feet* without moving from the *Spot*."

Cf. M. J. Chénier:

> C'est le bon sens, la raison qui fait tout—
> Vertu, génie, esprit, talent, et goût.
> Qu'est la vertu? raison mise en pratique.
> Talent? raison produite avec éclat.
> Esprit? raison qui finement s'exprime.
> Le goût n'est rien qu'un bon sens délicat,
> Et le génie est la raison sublime.

[2] Buffon. Similarly d'Alembert claims it as a triumph of his time that nothing is now said in poetry that is not sensible enough to be said in prose.   [3] See F. C. Green's charming *Minuet*, p. 27.

There is indeed little to add to Prior's picture of one besetting malady of his century, the very opposite to the malady of the century that followed it.

> Nor Good, nor Bad, nor Fools, nor Wise,
>   They would not learn, nor could advise;
> Without Love, Hatred, Joy, or Fear,
>   They led—a kind of—as it were:
> Nor Wish'd, nor Car'd, nor Laugh'd, nor Cry'd:
>   And so they liv'd: and so they dy'd.

How significant, behind its banter, is Gray's letter to Nicholls in 1769!—"And so you have a garden of your own and you plant and transplant, and are dirty and amused; are you not ashamed of yourself? Why, I have no such thing, you monster; nor ever shall be either dirty or amused as long as I live."[1] The eighteenth century produced the garden of Candide, as its commonsense substitute for the garden of Eden; but it remained, for the most part, too urban, as well as too urbane, to cultivate even gardens very freely. And what a bleak desert their formal walks could grow! "'Tis ridiculous to judge seriously of a puppet-show," writes the disillusioned old age of Lady Mary Wortley Montagu. "I have never yet seen anything serious that was not ridiculous," echoes Horace Walpole. "Ah!" repeats Mme du Deffand, who had passed a bored and passionless life only to fall in love, when blind and decrepit, with one who might have been her son, "je le répète sans cesse, il n'y a qu'un malheur, celui d'être né. Quelle cruauté de se marier, tirer des individus du néant! Tout ce qui existe est malheureux, un ange, une huître, peut-être un grain de sable; le néant, le néant voilà ce qui vaut le

---

[1] See Beer's *Eng. Romanticism in the Eighteenth Cent.*, p. 168.

mieux!'"'"Quant à moi," echoes Mme de Staal-Delaunay, as spring returns, "je ne m'en soucie plus; je suis si lasse de voir des fleurs et d'en entendre parler, que j'attends avec impatience la neige et le frimas." And he is no isolated figure, that pessimist of Thomson's *Castle of Indolence* who had found that the towers of Idlesse, like the gates of Reason, could not bar out the thin ghost of Ennui—

Ne ever utter'd word, save when first shone
The glittering star of eve—"Thank Heaven! the day is done."

Thus the natural Adam began to chafe under these silver chains of good sense and good taste. He longed to dream again. Enthusiasm—what the eighteenth-century peer who survived in Byron derided as "entusy-musy" and Landor, in this respect Byron's spiritual cousin, called "the hot and uncontrolled harlotry of a flaunting and dishevelled enthusiasm"—was, after all, too deep a natural need. It broke out from beneath the foundations of eighteenth-century sanity, as it has broken out again from under the foundations of nineteenth-century science and freedom of thought. First of all, the need to feel and express feeling showed itself in the growth of sentimentalism.

"You must not exhibit your feelings", said the code of *l'honnête homme*. "It is egotistic: *le moi est haïssable*." Thus a gentleman will be amusing; but he will not display his own amusement by a guffaw. Lord Chesterfield tells his son he cannot remember laughing since he had the use of his reason. "Do you never laugh, M. Fontenelle?" —"Non, je ne fais jamais *Ah-ah-ah*." Fontenelle never laughed, nor ran, nor wept; took to sitting on a stool without a back when he found himself stooping, towards ninety-eight; and died at a hundred, observing calmly—"Je ne sens autre chose qu'une difficulté d'être." But ordinary human nature could not live up to such standards. Men began to feel a chronic "difficulté d'être". Repression bred hysteria. The pocket-handkerchief was raised as the first banner of revolt—cautiously and whimsically at first by Sterne, who drops a single tear, as Recording Angel, to blot out Uncle Toby's oath; then wipes his Maria's streaming eyes; then finally howls aloud through the *Journal to Eliza*.[1] "Check not," says Sir Charles Grandison to the weeping bride, "check not the kindly gush." And after that the deluge. Madame de Francueil, for example, reads Rousseau's *La Nouvelle Héloïse* and weeps all day. An ill-dressed little man enters the room. She divines it to be the author himself; more tears—in which Rousseau partakes. Her husband tries heroically to make a jest; as well strike a match to dry the Atlantic; he too bursts into tears. And so for decades to come. "Tell dear George," writes Lady Granville of Byron's latest work, "that I think *Cain* most wicked, but not without feeling or passion. Parts of it are magnificent and the effect of Granville reading it out aloud to me was that I roared until I could neither hear nor see." A young man meeting Lamartine, so the poet himself relates, feels ill with emotion and sinks choking with tears into a chair. The young Victor Pavie describes meeting Victor Hugo and rushing into his arms—"Ici une lacune d'environ cinq minutes, pendant laquelle

---

[1] "I thought love had been a joyous thing", quoth my uncle Toby. "'Tis the most serious thing, an' please your Honour, (sometimes) that is in the world." *La Nouvelle Héloïse* and her impulsive sisterhood are already on the way.

je parlai sans me comprendre, sanglotant d'enthousiasme et riant de grosses larmes." It would be interesting to discover at what point in the nineteenth century the waters really receded.

To escape from the other tyranny, of the reality-principle, a number of eighteenth-century poets, as I suggested some years ago[1] and as has been pointed out again by Professor Housman, found it necessary, like the dog in Goldsmith's poem, to run mad. It was not for nothing that the sober Crabbe wrote, with a far-off and doubtless unconscious echo of Sophocles:

> The lame, the blind, and—far the happier they!—
> The moping idiot and the madman gay.

Gray was content with moping melancholia; but Collins is related to have run whining like a dog about Chichester Cathedral; Chatterton was odd and almost insanely megalomaniac, with madness also in his family; Smart went mad; Clare went mad; Cowper went mad, poor domestic tea-kettle singing thrust upon Hell-fire; Blake was not sane by ordinary standards; Shelley was eccentric; Byron neurotic to a degree; and opium has left its mark on the work of Crabbe, Coleridge and de Quincey. Like ivy on the tree it has strangled, like other parasites that perish in the completeness of their own triumph over their host, the sense of reality and the sense of social fitness were disintegrating at last.

There were two main lines of escape from over-civilized life—back to Nature and the Noble Savage and the secrets of the dreaming soul; or back to the Middle Ages. The former was the first to produce outstanding

---

[1] *Authors Dead and Living*, p. 93.

results—with Rousseau, that imprisoned vagabond who suddenly thrusts his fist through the window of the stifling *salon* and rushes lacerated and lamenting into the open air. He is, Amiel has pointed out, the ancestor or anticipator of half a dozen later types of writer—of the reveries of Chateaubriand, Senancour, and Wordsworth; of the natural descriptions of Bernardin de St Pierre; of the democratic theorists of the Revolution; of the educational theories of Pestalozzi; of the Romantic novel with its hyperbolic passions; of the nineteenth-century literature of the road and its literature of the Alps.

The other mediaeval escape was, I think, much less important than this return to being natural. Mediaevalism served merely as a favourite fancy-dress for the Romantic soul. But the revival of passionate dreaming went deeper than any revival of the past, though this side of Romanticism was the earlier to become prominent in England and Germany; leading from the Ballad collections of Philips, Ramsay, Percy, Bürger, and Scott; the forgeries of Chatterton and Macpherson; the Gothicism of Strawberry Hill and *Otranto* and *Götz von Berlichingen*, to the belated culmination of mediaeval mania in the France of *Hernani*—that strange world of *châtelaines*, all paled and slimmed (who could imagine a fat *châtelaine*?) and tricked out in *manches à gigot* and *toques à créneaux*, *aumonières* and *bijoux moyen-âge* (coronets or brooches embellished with good greyhounds or little footpages); while about them fluttered strange dandies calling themselves *Jehan* instead of *Jean*, wearing *chapeaux à la Buridan*[1] or *cheveux mérovingiens* or *cheveux*

---

[1] Readers of Villon will recall this legendary scholar thrown in a sack into the Seine.

en tempête, with Toledo blades by their sides and vast mediaeval pointed toes on their shoes. For if mediaevalism came late to France, it came with a vengeance; and its career there is a typical example of Romantic exaggertion and unreality. Even schoolboys were now dressed as pages with little daggers, soldered fast in the sheath for safety; even infants had cradles *à la Marguerite de Bourgogne*. Young men endeavoured to float companies for reviving the tourney; or formed societies like the so-called *Francs-Archers*, who came to an untimely end after they had brewed a too practically romantic scheme for abducting the *inamorata* of one of them. Even the *Dépôt des Estampes* suddenly found its venerable dust disturbed by an invasion of fashionable ladies, all burning to get their mediaeval costumes correct for the next ball and armed, to the librarian's horror, with authorizations from the minister to take his treasures out on loan. Or at midnight parties, while the flames flared blue in the punch-bowls, suddenly "Enter Yorick"—a skeleton in a Gothic armchair, who ventriloquently addressed the company. Some even shouted for Yorick to join in the dance; but Yorick's proprietor was so unromantically sordid as to object, for fear the thing's vertebrae might suffer damage.

But such fashions pass. With Hugo's *Les Burgraves* (1843) the Gothic ramparts of Romanticism collapsed before a battery of yawns. They were never the same again in France. In England, indeed, the Middle Ages could still inspire true poetry, in Pre-Raphaelite hands, as late as the seventies. But even in England little "mediaeval" work has been born and lived in the last fifty years. After a century the vein (only temporarily, no doubt) had exhausted itself.

But, to return, it was the psychological revolution that mattered. The essence of the Revival was that it now became reasonable to be irrational, and conventional to flout convention. The hatches of the Unconscious were once more unbattened. The literary effects of this have already been analysed; in poetry, if not in prose, they were mostly to the good; but its psychological effects were in the long run to prove less admirable. They were indeed to bring Romanticism at last into decadence and derision. It is at this point in its history that the Devil's Advocate must have his say.

"Le cœur le plus serein en apparence", writes Chateaubriand, long before the Unconscious was ever heard of, "ressemble au puits naturel de la Savane Alachua; la surface en paraît calme et pure, mais quand vous regardez au fond du bassin, vous apercevez un large crocodile." We have come to know more about the crocodiles of the Unconscious than Chateaubriand knew; and to believe that its depths contain more crocodiles than one. Many of the Romantics, especially in France, tried making pets of theirs; some got eaten by them; and many of their pages are wet with the crocodiles' tears.

Rousseau withdraws into solitude to dream. His friends are at once outraged. The self-sufficing solitary, Aristotle had said, is either a god or a beast. The eighteenth century was quite sure he must be a beast—"un méchant". "Tout homme réfléchi est méchant" retorted Rousseau. It was into the wilderness, Scott reminded Ballantyne, that Christ Himself went to be tempted of the Devil. We smile. But it must be admitted that the Romantics often sought seclusion not only because they

wanted to dream, not only because they had a passion
for Nature, but also because they had a passion for
themselves. And there, like a Upas tree in a wilderness,
that passion grew unchecked.

I have called Romanticism a revolt of the Unconscious.
One of the stages infants pass through, according to
Freudian theory, is that of being in love with themselves.
But of this infantile stage there remains an unconscious
memory; there is always a risk of neurotic regression to it.
The malady has been well named Narcissism. And
it becomes a plague among the Romantics, broodingly
withdrawn from the real world and their fellow-men.
Rousseau, Wordsworth, Chateaubriand, Byron, Lamartine, Vigny, Musset, Hugo—all show a self-absorption
that at times grows grotesque. Fortunately, even if they
lived like Narcissus, the loving Echo of their voices has
not died.

Rousseau, for example, is convinced of being a man
unique and apart. "Je ne suis fait comme aucun de ceux
que j'ai vus; j'ose croire n'être fait comme aucun de ceux
qui existent." When he falls in love, it is "la passion la
plus vive peut-être qu'aucun homme ait jamais sentie."
"Peut-être" is something. But even "peut-être"
vanishes elsewhere: "Moi qui me suis cru toujours, et
qui me crois encore, à tout prendre, le meilleur des
hommes." Yet Rousseau considers himself modest—
"Je crois que jamais individu de notre espèce n'eut
naturellement moins de vanité que moi." We may doubt
if ever man made more arrogant profession of humility.

"Méditations enchantées!" writes Chateaubriand,
"charmes secrets et ineffables d'une âme jouissant d'elle-
même, c'est au sein des déserts d'Amérique que je vous

ai goûtés à longs traits!...Lorsque, dans mes voyages, je quittai les habitations européennes et me trouvai pour la première fois seul au milieu d'un océan de forêts... dans l'espèce de délire qui me saisit, je ne suivais aucune route, j'allais d'arbre en arbre, à gauche, à droite indifféremment, et me disant en moi-même: 'Ici plus de chemins à suivre, plus de ville, plus d'étroites maisons, plus de rois, plus de présidents de République, plus de lois, et plus d'hommes....'"[1]

All his life René sat like a lonely eagle brooding, with at intervals some magnificent cry, over a world not worthy of him. "Si Napoléon avait fini avec les rois, il n'en avait pas fini avec moi." Or again, to quote one of his prefaces: "C'est l'homme beaucoup plus que l'auteur, qu'on verra partout: je parle éternellement de moi."[2]

Similarly, Blake has no qualms about considering one of his works "the Grandest Poem that this World contains" (true, it had been dictated by spirits); and we know from other sources that de Quincey was not altogether romancing when he said: "if you have reason to write a life of Lucifer, set down that by possibility, in respect to pride, he might be some type of Wordsworth".[3]

[1] See E. Faguet, *Dix-Neuvième Siècle*, "Chateaubriand".

[2] Cf. the malicious, but unerring stabs of Sainte-Beuve: "En général, M. de Chateaubriand est un peu trop disposé à s'étonner de sa destinée." (*E.g.* at Mycenae he thinks he has hit on the tomb of Clytemnestra: "Singulière destinée, qui me fait sortir tout exprès de Paris pour découvrir les cendres de Clytemnestre!") And again: "M. de Chateaubriand embrassait quelquefois son adversaire; mais sur le balcon." That voice would have been sadly lost if no multitudes had followed it into the wilderness to listen.

[3] Cf. Wordsworth's sudden remark at a large party: "Davy, do you know why I published *The White Doe* in quarto?" "No." "To show the world my opinion of it."

The egotism of Byron is fiercer and more deliberate[1];
Lamartine's more wistful—

> Lamartine ignorant qui ne sait que son âme;

Alfred de Vigny's sterner, yet as naïve. After his reception by the Academy, "How did you like my speech?"
asked Vigny of a friend. "A little long, perhaps.'" "Oh,
but I am not tired." Hugo, again, to a youth who said
he had been reading Goethe and Schiller, could reply:
"Mais à quoi bon? Je les résume tous." He allows his
mistress in her letters to compare him favourably with
Christ and to anticipate the time when mankind will
date their chronology, instead, from Victor Hugo—"Je
crois que si Dieu se montre jamais à moi, ce sera sous ta
forme." Even a modern dictator could hardly ask more.

In one of the most famous flights of the Romantic
school, the young Musset impishly likens the moon above
a tall chimney to the dot over an "i".[2] A habit of sur-
mounting their own ego with a lunatic halo was the

---

[1] Cf. Peacock's Mr Cypress: "Sir, I have quarrelled with my wife;
and a man who has quarrelled with his wife is absolved from all duty to
his country. I have written an ode to tell people as much, and they may
take it as they list". And Byron's own words: "neither the music of the
shepherds, the crashing of the avalanche, nor the torrent, the mountain,
the glacier, the forest, nor the cloud, have for one moment lightened the
weight upon my heart, nor enabled me to lose my own wretched identity
in the majesty, and the power, and the glory, around, above, and
beneath me".

[2] We may recall, too, the Doppelgänger obsession that haunted
Musset (like Rossetti)—

> Un jeune homme vêtu de noir,
> Qui me ressemblait comme un frère.

This hallucination really occurred to him; and might serve as yet
another symbol of Romantic egotism. Even when the Romantics meet
a ghost, it is still an *alter ego*.

common failing of the Romantics in general[1] (though we perhaps, as members of the only race, so far as I know, which is egotistic enough to use a capital letter for its first person singular, cannot be too critical).

True, literary men have seldom been humble; but they have in some ages shown more fear of their fellows' ridicule, less tendency to parade in public, like processions of sandwich-men, with bleeding hearts on every sleeve. Goldsmith, we know, was vain.

> And one, the happiest writer of his time,
> Grew pale at hearing Reynolds was sublime;
> That Rutland's Duchess wore a heavenly smile—
> "And I", said he, "neglected all this while!"[2]

But for all that, living in the age of "good sense" and "good taste", before bleeding hearts had become trump-cards, Goldsmith wrote *The Deserted Village*; not *The Deserted Goldsmith*. His great contemporary versified *The Vanity of Human Wishes*; not *The Vanity of Samuel Johnson*. The drawing of his own personality he left to another—Boswell. He has not lost by it.

And again how graceful by contrast with these egotists is that perfect lady of the eighteenth century, Rousseau's contemporary, Mme de Boufflers!—

> Il faut dire en deux mots
> Ce qu'on veut dire;
> Les longs propos
> Sont sots.

---

[1] The trait still persists. Cf. J. Renard, *Journal*, p. 929: "Coolus raconte que d'Annunzio, lors de sa première visite à Sarah Bernhardt, s'arrêta à quelques pas d'elle et dit, comme inspiré: 'Belle! Magnifique! D'Annunzienne!' Après quoi, il dit: 'Bonjour, madame'."

[2] Crabbe.

> Il ne faut pas toujours conter,
>   Citer,
>   Dater,
> Mais écouter.
> Il faut éviter l'emploi
>   Du moi, du moi,
>   Voici pourquoi;
> Il est tyrannique,
> Trop académique;
>   L'ennui, l'ennui
>   Marche avec lui.
> Je me conduis toujours ainsi
>   Ici,
>   Aussi
> J'ai réussi.

Naturally this new Narcissism becomes part of a vicious circle. Living on his feelings the Romantic grows more and more self-centred: the more self-centred he grows, the more he is reduced to living on his own feelings. His ego becomes his Universe; and only the fires of passionate excitement can prevent it from becoming a desert Universe of death and darkness. "The great object of life is sensation, to feel that we exist, even though in pain"—that Byronic cry is the keynote of one Romantic career after another. The "pain" was seldom slow to follow.

Those who seek such perpetual intoxication, must either vary the stimulant or increase the dose. Variation is sought by a growing cult for every kind of *bizarrerie*. Baudelaire, for example, calls on Maxime du Camp with his hair dyed green.[1] Maxime du Camp studiously ignores it. At last Baudelaire is driven to ask point blank —"Vous ne trouvez rien d'anormal en moi?"—"Mais

[1] There are now literary ladies in America, apparently, who dye theirs pink. D'Annunzio has appeared in a blue wig. So few ways are there of being original.

non."—"Cependant j'ai des cheveux verts, et ça n'est pas commun."—"Tout le monde a des cheveux plus ou moins verts; si les vôtres étaient bleu de ciel, ça pourrait me surprendre; mais des cheveux verts, il y en a sous bien des chapeaux à Paris." But Maxime du Camp was less successful in coping with a similar taste for oddities in his friend Flaubert, who once borrowed from a showman a five-legged sheep which had fascinated him, in order to let it loose in Maxime du Camp's bedroom when he was ill.

But tastes for green hair, blue roses, black mistresses, or five-legged sheep are comparatively harmless. Unfortunately there are not enough novelties in this world. The doses of excitement have to be increased as well as varied. Thus a young man to whom his parents have given the name of Théophile Dondey (actually they had not even called him Théophile), can juggle its letters into the more picturesque "Philothée O'Neddy". But what's in a name? Such thin excitements soon pall.

He finds it necessary to publish verses with some title like *Feu et Flamme*. But not even this can assure immortality. Where to-day is Philothée O'Neddy? With his forgotten and no less romantic peers—Augustus Mackeat (whose real name was Maguet) and Napoléon Tom and Jehan du Seigneur, with his extra "h", and Petrus Borel, "le lycanthrope", and Elias Wildmanstadius, "l'homme moyen-âge". The famous red waistcoat of Théophile Gautier, despite the moths of time, has outlived all these in the memories of common men.

And so it became necessary to go on and on from frenzy to frenzy. The novel of horrors, for example, had to plunge from skulls to skeletons, from skeletons to whole cemeteries. The worms of Monk

Lewis[1] grow tame beside the refinements of Poe.
Similarly love has to become a volcanic eruption.

> J'ai l'âme en feu, je suis volcan,
> Je brûle, je souffle, et je crache.[2]

Young Frenchmen of the period, learning that they
will be parted for three whole monstrous weeks from
their mistresses, rush out into woods, howling "comme
un démon"[3] and roll on the ground, grinding snapped-off
branches between their teeth. Suffice a description by
Berlioz of his own interview with Harriet Smithson
shortly before their marriage: "Il y a eu un reproche de
ne pas l'aimer; là-dessus, je lui ai répondu de guerre
lasse en m'empoisonnant à ses yeux. Cris affreux
d'Henriette!...désespoir sublime!...rires atroces de
ma part!...désir de revivre en voyant ses terribles
protestations d'amour!...émétique!...ipécacuana!...
vomissements de deux heures!...il n'est resté que deux
grains d'opium; j'ai été malade trois jours et j'ai survécu."[4]

It reads like a parody of the end of Emma Bovary.
No wonder that, scaling Vesuvius in eruption at midnight, the young musician felt, he says, face to face with
a brother-soul. No wonder gentlemen took to going
about with their hands pressed on their chests for fear
of a sudden physical explosion of so much pent-up
passion. And the violence, in France, of the ensuing
reaction against all this becomes also more intelligible.

---

[1] *E.g.* "Often have I, at waking, found my fingers ringed with the
long worms which bred in the corrupted flesh of my infants." This
Romantic obsession with physical horrors suggests other neurotic regres-
sions—sadism and necrophily.

[2] From a contemporary satire. L. Maigron, *Le Romantisme et les Mœurs*,
p. 145.

[3] From a letter written by the hero himself. Maigron, p. 153.

[4] Maigron, p. 155.

"De mon temps," obsérved an elderly gentleman in a tedious *salon* of 1850, "c'était plus amusant. De mon temps, Monsieur, nous traînions les femmes par la chevelure sur le parquet." Others were less regretful. It is clear that impulses exaggerated to this extent are approaching the definitely morbid—the point where we are faced not merely with exaggeration, but disease.

There was also the danger of insincerity. Men who pursue emotion for emotion's sake are tempted both to lash to hysteria the feelings they have, and to simulate feelings they have not. Thus Fontanes, the friend of Chateaubriand, trying to be as romantic as *Ossian*, performs the feat of becoming much more ridiculous:

> Que ne puis-je habiter les monts couverts de neige
> Où l'Écosse enferme ses citoyens heureux,
> Et contemplant les mers qui baignent la Norvège,
> Rêver au bruit des vents sous un ciel ténébreux!

Imagine the dismay of the gentle Fontanes, had some impish Arabian genie taken him at his word and deposited him in December at Cape Wrath.

Similarly, though Barry Cornwall could not even face a Channel passage, this did not deter him from writing:

> I'm on the Sea! I'm on the Sea!
> I am where I would ever be...
> I love (oh! how I love) to ride
> On the fierce foaming bursting tide...
> I never was on the dull tame shore
> But I lov'd the great sea more and more.

It is deadly for poetry, when the rage for feeling intensely fails as tamely as this; sometimes it was still deadlier for the poet, when it succeeded.

For often, indeed, this Romantic relaxation of control seems like a regression to childishness. The Romantic idealization of childhood, as in Traherne, Vaughan, Wordsworth, Hugo, Swinburne, Stevenson, and Walter de la Mare is not without significance. It too is part of the Romantic dreamer's flight from the harsh, drab world of adult life. The childishness of the Middle Ages or the childishness of the nursery—both alike are refuges from the present. Childhood renewed has been spoken of as the gate to Heaven; it can also prove the gate to Hell. This path of escape, followed up to a point, can be delightful; followed too far, it can end in morbid abnormality. Here we approach that region of Romanticism, grown decadent,

> Where all life dies, death lives, and nature breeds
> Perverse, all monstrous, all prodigious things.

Not only were many of the Romantics childishly self-absorbed. The movement gave rise to more sinister peculiarities, which lie behind Goethe's description of it as "disease"; to sadism and masochism, the pleasure of inflicting pain and the pleasure of having it inflicted; to the twilit horrors of Poe and the Satanism of Baudelaire.

Satanism is the rebellious cry: "Evil, be thou my good." It may be merely ludicrous, as in the Neapolitan lady who wished it were a mortal sin to drink iced sherbet; or in jaded persons who form societies of "Splendid Sinners" and dabble in Black Masses. Stolen waters are sweet and nothing so fascinating as the forbidden. Romantics have always loved a rebel.

> Talk to me not about the Book of Sin,
>   For, friend, to tell the truth,
> That is the book I would be written in—
>   It is so full of youth.[1]

[1] Hafiz (transl. R. le Gallienne).

Symonds, again, records how among the young Italians of the Renaissance in its decline it was so common to find a special thrill in seducing nuns, that this type of gallant acquired special names, like *monachini*. So at this period we hear of young French Romantics taking pleasure in dressing up their mistresses as nuns and reading breviaries with them. There was even a group that assembled on Sundays to worship Satan. Thus at a meeting in February 1846 were recited seven poems, one in praise of each of the Seven Deadly Sins.[1] A significant passage from the praise of Pride runs thus:

> L'obéissance est douce au vil cœur des classiques;
> Ils ont toujours quelqu'un pour modèle et pour loi.
> Un artiste ne doit écouter que son moi,
> Et l'orgueil seul emplit les âmes romantiques.

> The slavish Classic soul loves docile awe—
> To serve some master or some ordinance.
> An artist's self should be his only law—
> Pride alone fills the brave heart of Romance.

Other effusions from the same source are equally explicit:

> Divinité du Mal, viens à moi, je t'implore;
> Viens, détruis l'univers sous ton souffle empesté.

> Je voudrais m'enivrer de coupables délices,
> *Aux bourgeois abhorrés paraître original*,
> Pour les cœurs innocents inventer des supplices,
> Faire fleurir l'inceste en un sein virginal.

> Mon âme est un cloaque immonde où, sans émoi,
> Se tordent enlacés les plus hideux reptiles.

> *Sentir, je veux sentir à n'importe quel prix!*

[1] Maigron, p. 187. Cf. Swinburne's puerile fantasy of having seven towers in which to enact in weekly rotation the Seven Deadly Sins.

"Ah! tonnerre et sang!" writes a Jeune-France fired by seeing the *Anthony* of Dumas into out-ranting Shakespeare's Edmund, "Pourquoi suis-je légitime! Pourquoi ne suis-je pas bâtard!"[1]

Such impulses may be merely curiosities in the history of morals; but they have left their mark on the history of literature. This Satanic rebel recurs in Blake, in Schiller's *Robbers*, in the Novel of Horror, in Byron's Giaours and Corsairs and Laras and Manfreds and Cains and Don Juans.

> There was in him a vital scorn of all:
> As if the worst had fall'n which could befall,
> He stood a stranger in this breathing world,
> An erring spirit from another hurled.

He reappears, rather feebly, in the Octave of Stendhal's *Armance*; in Baudelaire; in Poe; in phrases of Swinburne about

> The lilies and languors of virtue,
>   The roses and raptures of vice;

in the haunted preoccupation of Rossetti with Sirens and lost souls; in Oscar Wilde and Aubrey Beardsley. Proust's Mademoiselle Vinteuil deliberately pursuing her Lesbianism in front of her dead father's photograph serves to show the persistence of the type. Even Alfred de Vigny's *Éloa*, the angel who of her tenderness falls in love with Satan,[2] is a nobler symbol of this recurrent tendency of the Romantic soul. From the prevalent fashion of Satanic mania, indeed, not even dogs were exempted. Readers of the Goncourts' journal may recall the dog of Rollinat, who had made the poor beast insanely

---

[1] Maigron, p. 104.
[2] Cf. Lamartine's *La Chute d'un Ange*.

Bohemian by beating it when it behaved well, and giving it sugar when it did not. How typical is the contrast between this Romantic pride in "the purity of their diabolicism" and the comment of the Prince de Ligne with his eighteenth-century good sense and good breeding on the blasphemies of Frederick the Great's conversation —"Il mettait un peu trop de prix à sa damnation."

What is the origin of such Satanism? This too seems one of the crocodiles of the Unconscious; this rebellion, this trampling on the ideal, may be in part another form of infantilism, of the so-called Oedipus-complex. Blake for example was not only the first to see in Milton's Satan the patron-saint of Romantic rebellion—so that "the true poet" is "of the Devil's party", even if like Milton he does not know it; Blake's own doggerel railings against God under the title of "Nobodaddy" (illuminating name) are as Oedipodean as any psycho-analyst could desire.

To Nobodaddy

Why are thou silent and invisible,
Father of Jealousy?
Why dost thou hide thyself in clouds
From every searching Eye?
Why darkness and obscurity
In all thy words and laws,
That none dare eat the fruit but from
The wily serpent's jaws?
Or is it because Secrecy gains females' loud applause?

Akin to this is the Romantic preoccupation with incest, as in earlier Romantics like Euripides and Ford, so in Walpole's *Mysterious Mother*, in *Laon and Cythna*, *The Cenci*, *René*, *Manfred*, and *Parisina*, and in Byron's own life; not to mention later works like d'Annunzio's

Città Morta. For incest itself is still pursuit of *La Princesse Lointaine*: none so impossibly remote, by the laws of society, as a man's closest kin. It is also the most fundamental of all rebellions against the Father.

But there are yet other crocodiles in the Unconscious, which the Romantic has sometimes invited out, to live with and on him. Among the most primitive of our impulses appears that lust for destruction which goes side by side with our passion to live. According to Count Keyserling, the Chinese with all their self-control are liable to fits of bull-fury about nothing—"The Chinese explain this phenomenon through the accumulation of the substance of anger, Ch'i". We may recall Aristotle's *catharsis* and Ibsen's pet scorpion, which used to grow ill unless given now and then a piece of fruit into which it could discharge its venom, so that Ibsen recognized in it a symbol of himself. As another poet has put it—

> The barest branch is beautiful
> One moment, while it breaks.

This delight in destruction, prominent at an infantile stage, may later develop and turn outwards as sadism, which tortures what it loves, or inwards, as masochism, which loves being tortured.

Now a learned work has been written by Dr Mario Praz, *La Carne, La Morte, e il Diavolo nella Letteratura Romantica*, which, taking for its text a sentence of Sainte-Beuve's, sees stretching across all Romanticism this monstrous shadow of the Marquis de Sade. It is a valuable and heavily documented book; but a great many of the authors dealt with are, after all, merely the pygmies of Romanticism. It is important not to exaggerate this element of perversion; but it must be

faced, because it provides another example of the part
played in Romantic literature by the less conscious
impulses of the mind; because the decay of Romanticism
was hastened by it; and because the good and bad in
Romanticism cannot be balanced without.

This strange fascination of suffering, this love of
Dolores, "Our Lady of Pain", is no invention of "the
divine Marquis" from whom it takes its name. Its presence
is already felt in plays like those of Seneca and some
Elizabethans, in novels like Nash's *Unfortunate Traveller*.
And the genial and enthusiastic Diderot, in more ways
than one a forerunner of Romanticism, already recognized it.

Of a statue of Cleopatra with her asp he writes:
"Les grands effets naissent partout des idées voluptueuses
entrelacées avec les idées terribles; par exemple de
belles femmes à demi-nues (*sic*) qui nous présentent un
breuvage délicieux dans les crânes sanglants de nos
ennemis. Voilà le modèle de toutes les choses sublimes.
C'est alors que l'âme s'ouvre au plaisir et frissonne
d'horreur." It is an odd idea; but it was one day to
become a common one and be put in practice, skulls
and all.[1]

Thus at the end of her mad affair with Musset,
George Sand buys a skull and encloses in it her lover's
last letter. A young lady calls one evening and leaves

[1] To Sophie Volland, 15. x. 1762. (Quoted in F. C. Green, *Minuet*.)
Cf. *De la Poésie Dramatique* (*Works* VII, 371), where Diderot speaks of
the romance of scenes, "où des pythies écumantes par la présence d'un
démon qui les tourmente, sont assises sur des trépieds, ont les yeux
égarés, et font mugir de leurs cris prophétiques le fond obscur des antres;
où les dieux, altérés du sang humain, ne sont apaisés que par son effusion."
We are reminded of Flaubert's *Salammbô* and D. H. Lawrence's *Plumed
Serpent*—neither, I feel, examples of Romanticism at its happiest.

a skull on Sainte-Beuve. Victor Hugo keeps a skull on
his mantelpiece as a more poetic way of recording time
than a clock. His Han d'Islande drinks sea-water from
a skull; and the young of the thirties sing—

> Nous allons boire à nos maîtresses
> Dans le crâne de leurs amants.

The whole Romantic rage for horrors, already men-
tioned as an instance of their craving for violent sensations in general, clearly owes some of its force to this
infantile lust for destruction and death in particular.
Berlioz at Florence meets a young woman's funeral in
the street, follows it, has the coffin opened, takes the
dead hand—"Si j'avais été seul, je l'aurais embrassée."
There even grew up a fashion for loving young women
because consumptive—

> Un démon de velours, une pensionnaire,
> Belle de deux défauts, gâtée et poitrinaire.[1]

Baudelaire approaches his mistress—

> Je m'avance à l'attaque, et je grimpe aux assauts
> Comme après un cadavre un chœur de vermisseaux.

There is no need to multiply this "wormy circumstance", nor to quote La Charogne, a poem still popular in
some circles. The malady is common enough. But a little
more must be said of the pleasure felt in inflicting pain.
A mania of this type is the simplest and most charitable
explanation of Byron's treatment in real life of Lady
Byron, from her wedding-day to the birth of their child.
It was not ordinary hatred for one of whom in other
moods he was fond, that cried on their honeymoon,
"I will live with you, if I can, till I have got an heir—

---

[1] Maigron, p. 180; who gives abundant other examples.

then I shall leave you"; and yet, at another moment, "You should have a softer pillow than my heart...". Before Ada's birth, he told Lady Byron he hoped she would die and the child with her; and, if it lived, he cursed it. And yet when his wife at last abandons him. he bursts into cries of rage and anguish.

A far clearer expression of this state of mind is found, once more, in Baudelaire; above all in the famous

C'est l'Ennui. L'œil chargé d'un pleur involontaire,
Il rêve d'échafauds en fumant son houka.

Similarly the heroine of Flaubert's *Madame Bovary*, which is not only a masterpiece, but also a perfect medical dictionary of Romantic maladies, after her phases first of Scott and knights-errant, then of sultans and minarets, sinks near the end to read "jusqu'au matin des livres extravagants, où il y avait des tableaux orgiaques avec *des situations sanglantes*". Swinburne was obsessed with the same impulse. Anyone who feels sceptical of its presence in *Atalanta* and *Anactoria*, *Phaedra* and *Faustine*, may speedily remove his doubts by a glance at the poet's puerile ecstasies over flogging in *Lesbia Brandon* or *The Whippingham Papers*. And those who wish for further examples of this disease of Romanticism will find them in Dr Praz, who points out—very acutely, I think—that this obsession with giving or suffering pain has produced two recurrent types in Romantic literature. First there is the sinister and daemonic male, like Anne Radcliffe's Montoni and Schedoni; the elder Cenci; Emily Brontë's Heathcliff with "his sharp cannibal teeth", his "yearning" for "crushing out entrails" and hanging dogs; Stendhal's Julien Sorel, who shoots his mistress in church; and some of the figures in Mérimée, Baudelaire, and Baudelaire's cherished Edgar Allan Poe. Here too Life took to aping Art; and Gautier has amusingly described the Romantic type of the thirties:

> J'étais sombre et farouche,
> Mon sourcil se tordait sur mon front soucieux,
> Ainsi qu'un vipère en fureur; et mes yeux
> Dardaient entre mes cils un regard ferme et louche;
> Un sourire infernal crispait ma pâle bouche.

To-day this sort of sadism once more reappears in D. H. Lawrence, whose lovers embrace their mistresses with hands red from killing rabbits, or genially reflect—

> Under the glistening cherries, with folded wings
>   Three dead birds lie;
> Pale-breasted throstles and a blackbird, robberlings
>   Stained with red dye.

> Against the haystack a girl stands laughing at me,
>   Cherries hung round her ears,
> Offers me her scarlet fruit: I will see
>   If she has any tears.

The counterpart of these male Romantic ogres, displacing them more and more as the movement grew more decadent and effeminate, was the female of the species—*La Belle Dame Sans Merci*. It is not wholly accident, I think, that the writer of that most perfect poem should also have written in real life to Fanny Brawne: "I have two luxuries to brood on, your loveliness and the hour of my death. Oh that I could have possession of them both in the same minute."[1] This type of the *femme fatale* reappears in his Lamia, in Mérimée's

---

[1] Cf. for the reverse side of this passion, his other phrase to her: "You must be mine to die upon the rack if I want you."

Vénus d'Ille, in the Cleopatras of Pushkin and Gautier, in the Salammbô of Flaubert and the Ennoia of his *Tentation de St Antoine*:[1] "Elle a été l'Hélène des Troyens, dont le poète Stésichore a maudit la mémoire. Elle a été Lucrèce, la patricienne violée par les rois. Elle a été Dalila, qui coupait les cheveux de Samson. Elle a été cette fille d'Israël qui s'abandonnait aux boucs.... Elle s'est prostituée à tous les peuples. Elle a chanté dans tous les carrefours. Elle a baisé tous les visages.... Innocente comme le Christ, qui est mort pour les hommes, elle s'est dévouée pour les femmes.... Elle est Minerve! Elle est le Saint-Esprit."

Here a familiar echo is heard, a familiar face appears—Pater's *La Gioconda*: "She is older than the rocks among which she sits; like the vampire, she has been dead many times, and learned the secrets of the grave...and as Leda was the mother of Helen of Troy, and, as St Anne, the mother of Mary".

It is amusing to detect from her accent that this versatile vampire had been also the Ennoia of Flaubert.[2] As a description of the fat and fatuous female who simpers from the canvas of Leonardo, one may find Pater's purple fantasy a little overwrought; it would make a far truer picture of the *Belle Dame Sans Merci* of Romanticism in general; who has found yet other incarnations in that Siren of Rossetti who sings in the apple-tree above the

[1] See Mario Praz, p. 212, and his whole chapter on *La Belle Dame Sans Merci*.

[2] Her form of utterance, indeed, is far older still. Cf. Taliesin: "I carried the banner before Alexander.... I was in Canaan when Absalom was slain.... I was in the hall of Don before Gwydion was born.... I was on the horse's crupper of Elias and Enoch; I was on the high cross of the merciful son of God; I was chief overseer at the building of the tower of Nimrod; I have dwelled three times in the castle of Arianrod...."

pit full of her lovers' bones; in Dolores and Mary Stuart
and many another heroine of Swinburne; in the Salome
of Mallarmé, Wilde, and Beardsley; in the Rebecca West
and Hedda Gabler and Hilda Wangel of Ibsen; in the
morbid ending of Flecker's *Hassan*; or in those films of
Greta Garbo which, with their magnificent Scandinavian
restraint, still bewitch a modern world that has turned
its back on poetry.

Sensationalism, Satanism, Sadism—these were the
three maladies of later Romanticism. They appear to
have gone further in France than here (though it must
be remembered that abroad Sadism is reputed a particularly English taste). Consequently, the reaction was
quicker and more violent there than in England. As in
politics, so in literature, France has always swung to
wilder extremes. In any case Romanticism had brought,
together with much that is immortal, an orgy of sensation
and senselessness. Flaubert, son of a great doctor and
himself half a Romantic, so that he could exclaim "I *am*
Emma Bovary", has made a masterpiece of his *post-
mortem* on dead Romance. And Baudelaire, its supreme
martyr, has written in a style of Classic purity its agonized
Nunc Dimittis.

It is worth dwelling a moment on this poem, *Le
Voyage*, which he might well have called "Odyssey", and
contrasting it with earlier Romantic treatments of the
same theme. For if Homer's *Odyssey* gives us the begin-
nings of Romanticism, this is indeed its bitter end. The
wine of the Romantic Dionysus is drunk—here are its
acrid lees.

Homer's Odysseus is warned by the spirit of Tiresias,

the prophet in Hades, that even when he has won his hearth again in Ithaca, he must one day set forth once more, with an oar on his shoulder, till he comes to men who so little know the sea that they mistake his oar for a winnowing-shovel. Now Homer's Romanticism is moderate and rational; not the daemonic restlessness it was one day to become; and so his Odysseus receives this prophecy with stoic silence and changes the subject. What must be, must be; so the gods have doomed.

Two thousand years later, the mediaeval imagination of Dante was fired by this idea of the old hero's final quest. Dante meets the soul of Ulysses drifting in a fireball, which eternally consumes it, along the Eighth Circle of Hell. For Ulysses is now damned on account of his too cunning stratagems on earth, such as the wooden horse of Troy. To Greek common sense such punishment for a legitimate and brilliant feint of war would have seemed completely crazy; but we are now in the Middle Ages, when men had more imagination than intelligence. Dante's Ulysses is accordingly far more Romantic than Homer's; he tells with superb eloquence how he was driven once more to sea by his passion to explore for exploration's sake. The Greek Odysseus would have felt this a strange lunacy. He had himself feigned madness, though in vain, to escape leaving home for Troy; not even *princesses lointaines*, though two of them were goddesses, could make him forget his longing to return; and so far was his very human common sense from the passionate *Wanderlust* of Dante's hero, that he wept aloud in Circe's bed and rolled about in speechless misery, when she told him he must first sail to Hades to consult Tiresias. And yet Dante's Ulysses becomes magnificent in his far wilder fantasy:

> nè dolcezza di figlio, nè la pieta
>   del vecchio padre, nè il debito amore
>   lo qual dovea Penelope far lieta,
> vincer poter dentro da me l' ardore
>   ch' i' ebbi a divenir del mondo esperto,
>   e degli vizii umani e del valore....
>
> "o frati," dissi, "che per cento milia
>   perigli siete giunti all' occidente,
>   a questa tanto picciola vigilia
> de' vostri sensi, ch' è del rimanente,
>   non vogliate negar l' esperienza,
>   di retro al sol, del mondo senza gente.
> considerate la vostra semenza:
>   fatti non foste a viver come bruti,
>   ma per seguir virtute e conoscenza."

Not fondness for my son, nor piety
    Towards my old father's years, nor yet the claim
    Of love that bade me cheer Penelope,
Could quell the passion in my heart aflame
    For gathering experience of the world,
    Of human greatness and of human shame...

"Brothers," I said, "since ye have reached the West
    Despite a hundred thousand dangers run,
    Waste not this little watch that now, at best,
Is left our eyes and ears, ere all be done;
    Lose not the knowledge of that world unknown,
    Unpeopled, but pursue the setting sun.
Consider of what seed ye have been sown,
    Who were not born to live your days like beasts,
    But to win worth and wisdom for your own."

So they sail out past Gibraltar, south across the line, and after five moons see looming up dimly like a greater Tenerife, the Mount of Purgatory; then God smites them and they sink. And yet that Dante should then complacently leave his hero roasting for eternity, is one of the things that make his genius seem to me as deformed as it was great.

The Romantic Revival had its own Odysseus—the Ancient Mariner. He too finds a Purgatory in the wastes of sea south of the line. But it is worth noticing that in parts, as where his hermit appears, with mossy oak-stump for cushion, Coleridge is more "mediaeval" than Dante himself; especially in his earlier version with its over-antiquated ballad-diction. He is also more romantically picturesque; for the poet has now become more sensitive to the background, the setting, the scenery, the appurtenances of his story. It is above all as a collection of seascapes that *The Ancient Mariner* lives. As in so much Romantic literature, the character of its hero remains shadowy. This reincarnation of Flying Dutchman and Wandering Jew is, indeed, almost Everyman. Coleridge's moral is more appealing than Dante's—it insists on pity even for animals, instead of eternal torture for human beings; though it remains not much more intelligent to condemn a whole ship's company to die of thirst because one of them has shot a bird. Coleridge himself came to feel that the moral was not quite happy; but, after all, it hardly matters. Romance is a dream, not a treatise on ethics. Some may find, indeed, that it is here a little too dreamy; that Coleridge is only writing a picturesque fantasy, where Dante was uttering in grim earnest the truth that was in him; that Poetry, in short, has here sunk from a gospel and a vision to an entertainment and a Quantock night's dream. But, when all is said, *The Ancient Mariner* remains an immortal miracle, an example of what we should have irreplaceably lost without the Romantic Revival.

From Dante Tennyson took up the tradition. With his *Ulysses* appears that reaction half-way to Classicism in which Tennyson and Arnold correspond to the French Parnassians. Tennyson's Ulysses is far less than Dante's a victim of blind irresistible impulse, like some migrant bird. He too longs, indeed,

> To follow knowledge like a sinking star
> Beyond the utmost bound of human thought.

And yet he lacks the superhuman, daemonic, Michel-angelesque mystery of Dante's hero, just because he tries to make his enterprise more rational and intelligible, by telling us, somewhat ungallantly, that Penelope is now old and his Ithacan subjects do not appreciate him. Dante's Ulysses went in spite of the ties of father, wife, and son—so overmastering was his mad desire; Tennyson's Ulysses goes because this elderly traveller feels bored at home and prefers, like Montaigne, to die moving. Even his hope of seeing "the great Achilles whom we knew", that symbol of the lost Arthur Hallam, while further humanizing his motives, divides them, weakens them, leaves them less majestic with mystery.

In fact, Tennyson's poem is an excellent example of the way in which the more Classical type of poetry can lose in intensity what it gains in intelligence and intelligibility. The Victorian Ulysses is a little too much posed in a conventionally noble attitude on the eve of "crossing the bar". Indeed the poem, fine as it is, does not seem to me comparable with *Tithonus*, where Tennyson's melancholy, passionate byond all reasoned consolations, utters its vain and agonized cry against mortality.

Baudelaire, before he wrote *Le Voyage*, had probably, I think, read Tennyson's *Ulysses*; he has at least an unmistakable echo of Tennyson's *Lotos-Eaters* in their land where "it seemed always afternoon". But Baudelaire, like Dante, is a voice from the deeps of Hell. He lacks Dante's directness; yet here, as in the *Inferno*, we listen to a voice in agonized earnest; not to a musical fantasia composed largely for art's sake, as with Tennyson and Coleridge. And though in inferior artists deadly earnestness can itself prove only too deadly, to the greatest it adds greatness.

In this poem Baudelaire has followed the Romantic primrose-path, to where it winds among deadly nightshade and black bryony—"les fleurs du mal"—out into the last abomination of desolation and disillusion.

> O le pauvre amoureux des pays chimériques!
> Faut-il le mettre aux fers, le jeter à la mer,
> Ce matelot ivrogne, inventeur d'Amériques
> Dont le mirage rend le gouffre plus amer?

> Alas, poor lover of lands unexplored,
> Drunk dreamer of Americas at will,
> Must he be put in irons, flung overboard,
> Whose mirage makes the salt deep bitterer still?

For all Eldorados are desert islands now—

> So, revelling, Imagination sails
> To find but a reef when dawn breaks on the sea.

Baudelaire's traveller knows that he can never satisfy his desire, never escape himself or the pursuing feet of Time. Dante's Ulysses found Purgatory; Baudelaire finds Hell. Indeed, like Marlowe's Mephistophilis he carries Hell with him. And like the Psyche of Apuleius, he finds that the Beauty of Proserpine is Death. This is his gloomy goal; not the loved Ithaca of Homer's simple sanity. Everywhere, for Baudelaire, among the jewelled idols of the East as among the churches of the West, winds "the weary pageant of Immortal Sin".

La femme, esclave vile, orgueilleuse et stupide,
Sans rire s'adorant et s'aimant sans dégoût;
L'homme, tyran goulu, paillard, dur et cupide,
Esclave de l'esclave et ruisseau dans l'égout.

Woman, vile slave with vain and vacant brain,
Smileless self-worship, self-love unrepelled:
Man, greedy tyrant, lewd, athirst for gain,
Slave of that slave, stream in that sewer held.

And so life remains for ever "Une oasis d'horreur dans un désert d'ennui". And yet the Romantic in him, like the Wandering Jew,[1] still cries for ever "Onward!", even when he sails not for China, but for the world below.

O Mort, vieux capitaine, il est temps! levons l'ancre!
Ce pays nous ennuie, ô Mort! Appareillons!
Si le ciel et la mer sont noirs comme de l'encre,
Nos cœurs que tu connais sont remplis de rayons.

Verse-nous ton poison pour qu'il nous réconforte!
Nous voulons, tant ce feu nous brûle le cerveau,
Plonger au fond du gouffre, Enfer ou Ciel, qu'importe?
Au fond de l'Inconnu pour trouver du *nouveau*!

Come, Death, old captain! Time to put to sea!
Up, anchor! Earth grows dull. Let us be gone.
Though black as ink both wave and heaven be,
Deep in the hearts you know, the light shines on.

Pour us your poison's comfort. For—so hot
This fire beats in our brains—we will pursue
Through the abyss—Hell, Heaven, it matters not—
Of the Unknown, the quest of what is New.

[1] One of the originals, it should be remembered, of *The Ancient Mariner*.

So ends, in the death and madness of this spectre-ship, the great Romantic quest for new emotions, new fantasies, new intoxications, pursued to its extremity. Here we have travelled far beyond Tennyson's *Gleam* or Arnold's *Scholar-Gipsy*: but farther along the same road. The business of poetry, said Johnson, is "to make new things familiar or familiar things new". The weakness of most Romantics was that they forgot this second half—forgot that man cannot live on nightingales' tongues and pigeons' milk alone.

And so the sense of reality, of the outer world, of the existence of society as well as the individual, soon came sweeping back, in Naturalism. The self-forgetful ecstasies of Bohemian romance were now to be replaced by the dispassionate accuracy of the scientist, the cult of the Unconscious by the cult of specialized concentration, the blue rose by the blue-book. Yet it cannot be said that this scientific industry of the Goncourts and Zola has left work to compare with the triumphs of Romanticism, in spite of all its faults.

No less natural, in poetry, was the reaction from Romantic emotionalism to the impassive Classic perfection of Leconte de Lisle and the Parnassians. But the Romantic wine still remained fermenting, though less furiously. Not only did Hugo, with his superb vitality, continue to dominate his country like a lonely lighthouse, even from his exile in Guernsey; the Symbolists in their turn became even more dream-like than their Romantic ancestors; and to-day the Surrealists have carried the cult of the Unconscious to its limit, writing automatically without allowing the intelligence to interfere at all. It is curious that some human beings can always be found to carry every experiment to its extreme on their own vile bodies, however unpromising it may appear to the eye of common sense. Still it at least enables others to profit by their experience; though the result is usually exactly what might have been foretold.

In England the decline of Romanticism was far more gradual than in France. The Spasmodics were soon over; but for Tennyson's *Maud* their very name would be forgotten now. But with the Pre-Raphaelites English Romanticism enjoyed a lovely St Martin's summer. It died finally of old age rather than of its own excesses as abroad. The poets merely grew gradually more decadent—Rossetti with his chloral, Swinburne with his half-adult eccentricities, Francis Thompson with his opium, the poets of the nineties with their liqueurs and languors. Until, by the date of Dowson, Romanticism is very tired indeed:

> In music I have no consolation,
> No roses are pale enough for me.

> I was not sorrowful, but only tired
> Of everything that ever I desired.

> Her lips, her eyes, all day became to me
> The shadow of a shadow utterly.

> With pale indifferent eyes, we sit and wait
> For the dropt curtain and the closing gate.

When Tennyson, like his Arthur, put to sea, he left hardly a Sir Bedivere behind.

> The knights were dust,
> Their good swords rust.

There remained the magic of Yeats; but the romance of Hardy was a disillusioned romance. To-day either soaking in the Unconscious has gone so far that the poet maunders unintelligible things in a corner; or we dabble in proletarian poetry and mechanized art, just as the Soviets attempted to make symphonies of steam whistles and dynamos, with no sirens allowed to sing but those of the factory. Similarly the fiction of the cultivated modern varies from excursions into "thinking with the blood", and getting drunk on it, to coldly or cynically scientific vivisections of the heart. And yet the world at large cares little for such literary fashions. There at least the Empire of Romance endures unshaken. It is fascinating, for example, to note the works advertised on the back page of a recent number of the *New York Herald Tribune Books Supplement*—a paper comparable to the *Times Literary Supplement* in England. They are largely by well-known authors; and I have seldom seen a document that gave a more vivid epitome of the tastes and interests of modern man. The page begins with a flourish, in large type, recommending—"The Playboy Killer of Pagan Rome Who Sang Himself to Death. Son of a She Devil! Never has there ruled such a creature as this red-haired Singing Emperor! He delighted in burning and torturing Christians—fed them to his lions. Then his jaded passions sought new thrills in unspeakable practices... colorful despot...Arthur Weigall minces no words... read the shocking truth...slaughter that would have made a cannibal blanch!" How little mankind has changed since Monk Lewis!—except perhaps to grow yet vulgarer. "Marie Antoinette," the list continues, "notorious queen whose frivolity, extravagance and scandal ended on bloody guillotine"; "Napoleon"; "Nudism in Modern Life"; "New Book of Etiquette";

"The Story of Money"; "Astronomy for Everybody"; "Catherine the Great"; "On Going Naked. Adventures of young woman who turned from the private to public practice of nakedness"; "Strategy in Handling People"; "Among the Nudists"; "The Crusades"; "The Flame of Islam"; "Casanova"; "Sappho of Lesbos"; "Genghiz Khan"; "Marc Antony"; "Queen Elizabeth—Amazing era of Virgin Queen who built empire, died of heart-break"; "Is *That* in the Bible? A thousand curious, surprising items"; "Oscar Wilde"; "The Story of Mankind"; "Great Men of Science"; "The Human Body"; "Tamerlane the Earth Shaker"; "The Conquest of Happiness, by Bertrand Russell. Strips the shame from 'sin' and 'love'." Such are the present interests of our great world; some science, a little religion, a great deal of sex, and, still, unlimited Romance. And here as ever appear those three attendant evil spirits of Romance, like the three witches dancing round Macbeth—Sensationalism, Satanism, Sadism. Nero by himself bestrides half the entire page of the above advertisement. Here are still the same itch for destruction, the same fascination for men of terror, like Marlowe's Tamerlane and Genghiz Khan and Napoleon; for women of fate, like Cleopatra and Agrippina and Catherine of Russia. And note that here we are not dealing with that main stronghold of Romance, the novel; these are its mere outposts—biography and history, so-called.

Or, again, turn to the current title-index of English published books and look up "Romance". The titles that comprise the magic word take up two whole columns of ironic juxtaposition. "The Romance of the Animal World" jostles "The Romance of the British Museum" and is followed by the "Romances" "of Coal"—"of the Cotton Industry"—"of Commerce"—"of Electricity" —"of Fish Life"—"of Great Businesses"—"of Insect Life"—"of King Arthur"—"of Leonardo"—"of Lighthouses"—"of the Machine"—"of Marriage"—"of Mary the Blessed"—"of Million Making"—"of Missionary Heroism"—"of Monte Carlo"—"of the Moon" —"of the Motor Car"—"of Piracy"—"of Poaching in the Highlands"—"of the Post Office"—"of Preaching"—"of Soho"—"of Sorcery"—"of the Sun"—"of Trade"—"of Tristram and Iseult". What a romantic world we appear to live in! What does it mean? That the human craving for intoxication is as insistent as ever and these authors are promising to gratify it by making the British Museum look like the palace of Queen Mab and the Post Office like Avalon—promises perhaps easier to give than to perform.

As in literature, so in life. Romanticism is the gin on which dictators like Hitler and Mussolini still fuddle the fools that acclaim them. "Better live three days as a lion than a hundred years as a sheep"—the youth of a nation repeats it, thrilled. The intelligence is lacking that should have smiled at the idea of "lions" advancing to massacre a half-armed enemy, under cover of gas and armour-plated tanks. A d'Annunzio can still write, urging the young to battle, screaming that the memory of Adowa is like a brand upon his shoulder. Similarly, a few hysterical sentences about Nordic heroism and Aryan purity suffice to build up a whole dream-world, in which a Hitler youth seems to himself a very Galahad as he spits on defenceless Jews.

Romanticism has fallen indeed.

NOTE

A recent work, Mr D. Gascoyne's *Surrealism*, which has reached me just as this goes to press, provides some interesting examples of the Romantic revolt of the Unconscious carried to its extreme and become quite conscious. The Romantic affinities of Surrealism are admitted. Among its ancestors it claims Shakespeare, Marlowe, Coleridge, Blake, Beddoes, Nerval, Baudelaire, and Huysmans. And here once more there rises "the enormous and sinister figure of the Marquis de Sade". Surrealism cannot, I think, be called "Romantic"; but it might well have been called Super-Romanticism; it stands to it as ultra-violet to violet.

Its immediate predecessor was "Dada"—for so the Roumanian Tristan Tzara christened his new movement, by opening a dictionary at random, in a Zürich café in 1916. Dadaism was simply an intellectual anarchism, in revolt against reason and everything else, and expressing itself in ecstasies of Tzara's like—

> In your inside there are smoking lamps
> the swamp of blue honey
> cat crouched in the gold of a flemish inn
> boom boom
> lots of sand yellow bicyclist
> chateauneuf des papes
> manhattan there are tubs of excrement before you.
> mbaze mbaze bazebaze mleganga garoo.

The Dadaists gave soirées where persons danced dressed in stove-pipes or announced that they would pull their hair out in public; or they held exhibitions to which the entrance led through a public lavatory, while hatchets were provided for the public to attack the exhibits, and a young girl, dressed as for her first communion, recited obscene poems (cf. p. 111). Similarly Marcel Duchamp sent in a lavatory-basin, entitled "Fountain", to the New York *salon*; and exhibited in Paris a printed reproduction of the Mona Lisa which he had wittily adorned with large moustaches and inscribed "LHOOQ" (Look!).

In 1922 Dada, amid much tumult, died in giving birth to Surrealism. Where Dada had been a negative rebellion of adolescent whimsicality, Surrealism deliberately set out to release the Unconscious and to create with the automatism of a dream, "in the absence of all control exercised by the reason and outside all aesthetic or moral preoccupations". "In surrealism one relives the best of childhood."

But, though it had acquired a theory for its infantilism, the new movement seems to differ little in practical results from the old. It has produced portraits made of blotting-paper, nibs, and needles; pictures pasted together from pieces of catalogues or newspapers; games worthy of the Mad Hatter, in which answers are given to questions that the answerer is not allowed to hear; films such as *The Golden Age*, in which "The erotic parts reach a high pitch of violence, culminating in a scene during which a flaming fir-tree, an enormous agricultural implement, an archbishop, a giraffe, and some feathers are all flung out of a bedroom window at the top of a house. Other details include the ill-treating of a blind man, a dog being run over, a father killing his son on the spur of the moment, and an old woman having her face slapped." The movement has also created proverbs, such as "All that fattens is not soft", or "A corset in July is worth a horde of rats"; and highly modern poems like the following:

The quarrel between the boiled chicken and the ventriloquist
had for us the meaning of a cloud of dust
which passed above the city
like the blowing of a trumpet.
It blew so loudly that its bowler-hat was trembling
and its beard stood up on end
to bite off its nose....

With their general tendency to hate and destruction the Surrealists show also a particular animus against "the bourgeois" (cf. p. 111) that has led them to hold out a hand to the Communists; who seem to have remained, however, coldly suspicious.

Here, in fact, that element of "disease" which Goethe found, surely with injustice, in all Romantics, utters its death-rattle; but it is not without interest, I feel, to find views of the relation of Romanticism to the Unconscious and the infantile, which I had originally formed in complete ignorance of Surrealism, to such an extent confirmed by the theory and practice of this its latest aberration.

CHAPTER III

FAIRIES AND FUNGI; OR THE
FUTURE OF ROMANTICISM

SUCH seems to me the essential history of Romanticism
and its maladies. It begins, before European history,
with the mythology of Greece—the dream-tales of a race
in its childhood. It recurs to some extent in Greek literature, though chastened by Greek sanity and self-control;
to a still smaller extent in the more matter-of-fact and
state-minded literature of Rome; until it revives as the
shadows of mediaevalism begin to fall. The Middle Ages
are its Golden Age. So far, in the *Odyssey* or the *Arabian
Nights* or *Aucassin and Nicolette*, Romance remains the
healthy day-dreaming of a young imagination, not so
much trying to escape from common life as to enhance
it—as natural and normal as the dreaming of a dog that
imagines itself hunting some perfectly celestial rabbit.
Homer's hearers had themselves faced battles and
tempests, though less marvellous than his; Malory, like
his own Sir Tristram, was a good knight in prison.

The Renaissance tended to look scorn on the rags of
mediaeval romance. Still it attempted compromise in
Tasso and Ariosto, in Ronsard, in Spenser and Shakespeare. But the compromise collapsed. The mediaeval
world became identified with superstition, intolerance,
barbarism and folly; it was hunted into an obscure grave
before the disciplined onmarch of modern science and
ancient culture. When the great reaction came, the new

Romanticism of the Revival was inevitably a more self-conscious and theoretic thing; more of an artificial intoxicant, less of a natural day-dream. Like Theocritus or Apollonius Rhodius in ancient Alexandria, so now Chateaubriand and Coleridge, Scott and Morris call up an imaginary world to redress the drab balance of the real. Keats dreams in Hampstead of stout Cortez in Darien. Men come to look to fantasy for emotional outlets that life has begun to deny. They project themselves into existences simpler or more adventurous than their own, minds unsicklied by analysis and balanced by active bodies and resolute wills. This type of Romanticism may be likened to a healthy use of wine. The Romantic drinks: he is not yet a drunkard.

But that too was to come. Writers begin to seek the hysterical over-stimulation of emotions normal in themselves, as can be seen in George Sand or D. H. Lawrence; the Romantic now drinks to excess. They begin also to seek the stimulation of emotions not normal at all; the Romantic becomes a drug-fiend, distilling "fleurs du mal". Like Narcissus, many of them had grown self-centred, making a god not merely in, but of, their own image; obsessed by their own reflections in the dark pool of personality. To liven the images they sought for sensations to stir the pool. But the spirits that came to trouble the waters for them, were often far from angelic; and in those unconscious depths lurked shapes far from angelic either. Once more reaction was inevitable. To-day Romanticism is no doubt only too much alive still in its less admirable forms; but what future has it in serious literature?

That it should have come under a cloud is in itself nothing. The law that literary fashions change is one of the few critical laws—almost the only one—that really hold. All stimulants lose their force with custom. The goddess Novelty is one of the immortals. Her handiwork is everywhere. The other day in a remote part of Cornwall I noticed she had produced a new kind of tea-cup with a square base instead of a round one, fitting into a square depression in the saucer. Naturally, it required great care and concentration to put it down so that it should fit at all. It had every reason of common sense against it. But it was new. That sufficed.

Yet we cannot be sure that all past fashions will necessarily return with the regularity of Halley's comet. Comets sometimes get lost. Human nature is always changing. Nature itself, which antiquity filled with gracious or terrible beings in its own image, for us grows less and less anthropomorphic, more impersonal, more automatic. Where the Greeks saw Olympus, we see a sort of infinite generating station. The Tibetans pray with wheels: but it is harder to pray to them.

And while Nature loses her personality, we tend by analysis to break up our own. Thinking always of his thoughts, scrutinizing his feelings, the modern man finds it ever harder to be carried out of himself by emotion or by dreams. He loses the gift of Romantic ecstasy. He begins to remember even in passionate moments that he did not view things so yesterday, and will not to-morrow. Such sincerity makes it harder and harder to be sincere. The wild impulses that once sprang or soared like wild things in a wilderness, grow shy with the sense,

now, of the watching eye of another self always upon
them.

> She had been beautiful in that old way
> That's all but gone; for the proud heart is gone,
> And the fool-heart of the counting-house fears all
> But soft beauty and indolent desire.[1]

While the many reel back into hysteria, the *sécheresse*
of the eighteenth century threatens the few. Calvin
Coolidge returns from church. "What did the preacher
talk about?" asks that strong silent man's wife. "Sin."
"And what did he say about it?" "He was against it."
In minds more intelligent there reappears to-day the
same malady as shows itself in the arid pages of Benjamin
Constant's *Adolphe* or in Madame de Charrière's rela-
tions with its author—lovers probing and dissecting their
own dry hearts into dust. "More and more, as I grow
older," wrote de Tocqueville, "I respect the passions,
even bad. They are at least a force." "Man is only truly
great," echoes Disraeli's Sidonia, "when he acts from
his passions; never irresistible but when he appeals to
the Imagination. Even Mormon counts more votaries
than Bentham." This is but too true. A D. H. Lawrence
makes far more proselytes than a Hardy or a Proust.
Faith can move mountains. Unfortunately it usually
drops them on other people's heads. Such are the evils
of too much passion, or too little: but it is even worse,
perhaps, to have too little than too much. And that is
the modern intellectual's danger.

What is the remedy? It is easy to talk of "turning
and living with the animals", of "thinking with the

---

[1] Yeats, *The Old Age of Queen Maeve.*

blood", or of going even a step further in the company of
Mr Yeats and thinking with the marrow.

> God save me from those thoughts men think
> In the mind alone,
> He that sings a lasting song
> Thinks in a marrow bone.
>
> I pray—for fashion's word is out
> And prayer comes round again—
> That I may seem, though I die old,
> A foolish, passionate man.

So Romantic in his old age remains our greatest living
poet. But can we thus self-consciously revert to the
Unconscious? "Je n'ai pas su me simplifier", cries
regretfully Turgeniev's helpless Nejdanof. It is no longer
easy to be simply wise and wisely simple. And yet, as
Bertrand Russell says, when intellectuals question if life
be worth living while gardeners feel no doubt of it,
it looks as if intellectuals had still something to learn from
gardeners; for, so long as life seems worth living, worth
living it is.

Life and literature are an eternal tight-rope walk.
Balance is essential. To the question "Classic or Romantic?" the answer is surely "Both". As Herrick and
Milton realized when they praised the loveliness of
poetry with paradoxes about "wild civility" or "wanton
heed and giddy cunning". The pure Classic is too stiff
and stifled; the pure Romantic too drunken and way-
ward; the pure Realist too drab; the Surrealist a self-
segregated sot. Classicism, Romanticism, Realism are
three extremes, three points of a triangle; the magic
circle lies inscribed within it. There move Homer and
Aeschylus, Virgil and Tacitus, Chaucer and Ronsard

and Shakespeare. Nearer the edge are writers like Racine and Hugo and Ibsen; outside it, the too heroic tragedy of the seventeenth century, the too Classic tragedy of the eighteenth, the too realistic novels of nineteenth and twentieth. The golden mean is hackneyed; but, like gold, it does not grow rusty. Blake might exclaim impatiently of Reynolds—

> He has observed the golden rule
> Till he's become the golden fool.

But Reynolds' pictures last quite as well as Blake's. He may write, with typical tantrums: "The Greek and Roman Classics is the Ante-Christ. I say Is and not Are as most expressive and correct too." But the Classic writers and English grammar still survive. "He really saw these things", Rodin was told, as he looked at some drawings by Blake. "Yes," came the answer, "but he should have seen them three or four times." He did not see them steadily or whole. Stendhal shows more understanding of both needs; writing at one time: "Ce que j'ai le plus aimé, c'était la rêverie"; and, at another, "Si je ne vois pas clair, tout mon monde est anéanti." But even Stendhal often fails to hold his balance; so that his novels oscillate from the confines of melodrama to the dryness of the *Code Napoléon*.[1]

There is in fact a time to dream and a time to wake; a time to remember reality and a time to forget it; a time to be drunk and a time to be sober; a time to "think with the blood" and a time to think with the brain. But none of these to excess. The Greeks knew it; that is why there

---

[1] It is typical that Stendhal should have been badly upset in the middle of a Napoleonic battle by a general who was so tritely romantic as to exclaim: "C'est une bataille de géants".

is so much that is Romantic in their so-called classics. Apollo did not burn the worshippers of Dionysus; he gave his young brother a share in his own Delphic shrine.

But can this balance be attained by calculation? Classicism, indeed, in its self-consciousness is largely a matter of taking thought; Realism, with its semi-scientific study of reality, can also be pursued, as by Scott, even, or Charles Reade or Zola, with notebooks; but the third ingredient, Romanticism, spontaneous feeling, the release of the Unconscious—can this wild growth too be cultivated? Good love poems, said Pope's friend Walsh, require that a man should be in love, to write them, and out of love again to correct them. But who can *will* to be in love?

Yet something can be done, I think, to cultivate even Romantic spontaneity. It is at least possible to avoid repressing it, to refrain from fussy over-precision. Castiglione makes a certain recklessness part of perfect manners. Luther, who was not overmuch concerned with good manners, notices, "when I am angry, I can pray well and preach well". "One must let one's pen trot as it will," writes Mme de Sévigné, "la mienne a toujours la bride sur le cou." The Prince de Ligne, defining *amabilité*, besides gaiety and grace and a dozen other qualities, insists on "de la négligence". They were wiser than Lord Chesterfield, who boasted that for forty years he had never used a word without reflecting if there were not a better one. I remember Mr Yeats once telling how his father warned him to write "like a gentleman"—that is, with a certain care-free ease. Stevenson has urged that a writer should alternately work hard and play; and that his best work will be done as play. Ruskin was equally certain that the best work is done easily, though only after painful apprenticeship. He might have instanced Dryden, whose later verse partly owes the masterly grace of its couplets to the thousands he had previously written in largely detestable dramas; or the Rossettis, who wrote so well partly as the result of composing endless sonnets to *bouts-rimés* as a children's game; or Sainte-Beuve, whose *Lundis* were so good, it has been said, because he had no time to spoil them. Anatole France, though he put his own work through eight sets of proofs, regretted that Flaubert did not do some journalism which would have compelled him to write fast. Another countryman of Flaubert's has told me that his letters are better written than the novels that cost such agony. I find it hard to believe in any style more perfect than that of *Madame Bovary*; but it is significant that this other opinion should be possible.

In fact, your art will seem natural, when it has become second nature. Even in tennis, many must have noticed how conscious concentration can never give the effectiveness of an instinctive stroke. Concentrated effort may help by long practice to build up this reflex skill; it can never equal it. And with mental problems or invention it is a commonplace that unconscious incubation can work wonders, where deliberate brain-racking brings not an idea, only a headache. Ideas, indeed, often seem to come creeping out like rabbits, in the stillness of idle meditation or when the attention is absorbed by some quite different book or task. So that Scott found it always better to have two or even a dozen irons in the fire at once.

No doubt this can be exaggerated. It is easy to dream too much. The Romantics often did. "L'artiste", writes Alain, "doit méditer *en poussant son outil*." But this also is too simple a generalization. Artists differ. Rousseau could never compose with pen in hand, nor Chateaubriand without. The wisest way was surely Virgil's, who began each day with many lines written in haste and ended with a few polished at leisure. But the fact remains: men can cultivate spontaneity instead of deliberately cramping it. This truth at least the Romantics have taught us. We are not wise if we deny ourselves this power of being wiser than we know.

It follows that it is also wiser to avoid too much criticism and self-criticism, that influenza of modern intellectuals—pale library-Hamlets who can never shut their querying eyes and leap. Amiel wails that he has hamstrung himself by too much of it. Flaubert echoes him. Rémy de Gourmont denounces passionately the fatuity of Apollo's injunction "Know thyself". They too exaggerate. But the danger is real. How many modern poets have sunk to become critics and never risen again!

But can we do more than this to preserve Romance as well as spontaneity, even in this age of prose and science? I think so. But here success depends on a view of life and a way of living; on a certain sanity and a certain health, dependent in their turn upon each other.

First, for the view of life: science, it is true, has destroyed the Dryad. The fairy-ring it has proved to be the work, not of fairies, but of fungi. And so Keats quite understandably drank confusion to Newton who had ungoddessed the rainbow; as he laments in *Lamia*,

> For the sage,
> Let spear-grass and the spiteful thistle wage
> War on his temples. Do not all charms fly
> At the mere touch of cold philosophy?
> There was an awful rainbow once in heaven:
> We know her woof, her texture; she is given
> In the dull catalogue of common things.
> Philosophy will clip an Angel's wings,
> Conquer all mysteries by rule and line,
> Empty the haunted air, and gnomed mine—
> Unweave a rainbow, as it erewhile made
> The tender-person'd Lamia melt into a shade.[1]

But Science, going further, has partly restored what she took away. The rainbow, she has said, is not a winged goddess; it is a matter of light-waves; Iris is a myth. But, going further, she has added: "But the waves also are a myth, a symbol, a way of schematizing certain sensations we feel and measure". As the world about us becomes more and more an unsubstantial pageant of dreams, our dreams become again, relatively, much more substantial. The Aphrodite and Artemis of the *Hippolytus* of Euripides cannot ever be as real again to men as they were to Greek piety; but, as marvellously vivid symbols of passion and the hatred of passion, they remain, even now, as real for us as a Universe that has itself become only a dance of phantom formulae on the

---

[1] It is surprising to find even Voltaire feeling this:

> On a banni les démons et les fées:
> Sous la raison les grâces étouffées
> Livrent nos cœurs à l'insipidité.
> Le raisonnement tristement s'accrédite;
> On court hélas! après la vérité;
> Ah, croyez-moi, l'erreur a son mérite.

points of dial needles. Man cannot bind the sweet
influences of the Pleiades nor loose the bands of Orion;
but man has named them and his own faculties colla-
borate to give them all the qualities they seem to possess.
As the flaming walls of Lucretius' world crumble and
fall to dust, we are forced back into the straitened
central citadel of our own sensations. There the Spirits
of the Pities, the Spirits Ironic of Hardy's *Dynasts* remain
symbols as true as the casualty lists of Trafalgar and
Austerlitz—and much more living. Well might Hardy,
in his marvellous old age, write on the one hand lines on
Relativity:

> That there's no time, no space, no motion,
>   Nor rathe, nor late,
>   Nor square, nor straight,
> But just a sort of bending ocean;

and at the same time lines on the relativity of Relativity
itself:

> If I have seen one thing
> It is the passing preciousness of dreams;
> That aspects are within us.

The Science of the nineteenth century seemed to expel
Poetry with a brandished test-tube; the Science of the
twentieth reopens the door to her with a bow. To quote
again from a letter of Hardy's in 1901: "I do not think
there will be any permanent revival of the old transcendental ideals; but I think there may gradually be developed an Idealism of Fancy; that is, an idealism in which
fancy is no longer tricked out and made to masquerade
as belief, but is frankly and honestly accepted as an
imaginative solace in the lack of any substantial solace
to be found in life." We may recall that other great
writer of our time, as obsessed as Hardy with Time

and Transience—the author of *A la Recherche du Temps Perdu*—and remember how, sitting in the restaurant at Rivebelle, Proust suddenly sees it as a mediaeval universe, its round tables as planets, its waiters as other heavenly bodies wheeling in their orbits, its *caissières* as two witches busily performing the astrological calculations that keep this celestial world in its courses, clear of catastrophe; and suddenly he pities the other diners who are absorbed, not in such fantasies, but their menus or their bills. This is, after all, only the attitude of Blake with his double vision, seeing a thistle as a greybeard by the wayside, the sun as a heavenly host crying Holy, Holy, Holy!

Yet there is a difference also; and it seems to me important to guard against extravagance in this view of life and literature. For it has been recently argued that, all science and knowledge being merely a methodical mythology, truth only matters or means anything in practical affairs, such as avoiding a motor-bus, where error means broken ribs. Poetry, it is urged, remains completely free of fact. Different poems are the means of assuming different "emotional attitudes"; and the more the merrier. Each is a different drug, giving a different dream; a new enchanted cigarette in a foggy world where all is smoke. The literary connoisseur can become all things to all gods; literature serves as a sort of combined camel and mirage to carry him across the Waste Land of modern life. It is very curious, this latest revival of Romanticism in a mystical disguise.

Such a divorce of literature from practical living seems to me rather dangerous mysticism. Literature, like life, is still vitally concerned with truth and falsehood, fact and fiction. There is always a motor-bus somewhere on the landscape. Even poetic "attitudes" have their own consequences, like any other event. We may carry the Universe inside our own skulls; it remains no less relentless. To let the reality-principle be intoxicated by the imagination is still just as unhealthy for life and letters as to let the romancing imagination be stamped out by a slavish sense of reality.

For even sensations lead to other sensations. Pursuit of the sensation of being drunk leads to the sensation of having a headache. Pursuit of the sensations of Romantic ecstasy has often led to other sensations of abject misery. The literature we read moulds, insensibly but inevitably, our sense of values; our sense of values moulds all we do and are. Fletcher of Saltoun believed that the ballads of a nation mattered more than all its laws. Plato might have been inclined to agree. Imagine your thistle by the wayside is an old gentleman, if you like; but if you then drop pennies into its hat you will be wasting your money. Let the moth desire the star; safer, very often, than desiring candles; but let it remember something of astronomical distances also, like the charming eighteenth-century Earl of Albemarle, our ambassador at Paris, who, seeing his Lolotte gazing up at a star, said to her: "Ne la regardez pas tant, ma chère; je ne sçaurois vous la donner." That too is poetry. It is also sense. I loathe this view of literature as a shelf of bottles each with a different brand of alcohol inside, on which to soak in secret. I like Blake often; but I like Hardy better. He did not muddle one kind of dreaming with another. I like minds that have also in them a spirit ironic that refuses to be too much swept away—like Sheridan, when he spoilt Burke's histrionic flinging of

a dagger large as a carving knife on the floor of the
House of Commons with the dry query—"Where's the
fork?"

> But play no tricks upon thy soul, O man;
> Let fact be fact, and life the thing it can.

Those lines of Clough, poor Romantic who was so
afraid of the tricks of romantic intoxication that he
lived an unhappily sober life, still keep their truth.
Clough forewent a good deal; but, to twist another phrase
of his, "'Tis better to have thought and lost than never
to have thought at all." Play tricks with your imagination
by all means; but know when they are tricks.

All great artists, thought Michelangelo, should have
some practice in architecture. It is an excellent antidote
to "emotional attitudes". Try certain architectural
attitudes for what you build and the laws of gravity will
inexorably break your neck and other people's. To me
the pleasure of literature is double—sharing a writer's
experience, and comparing it with my own. And the
pleasure is keenest when a voice within me cries not only
"How fine!" but also "How true!" That is why Hardy
is to me, as a poet, worth many Shelleys. Hardy was
a master builder, who had built houses that stood;
whereas Shelley's handling of material things only
landed him at the bottom of the Gulf of Spezzia. A sense
of reality is far from being everything; but it remains
for me a very great thing, even in imaginative literature.

In fine, Romanticism has been condemned as lacking
alike truth and health. It can be answered that all
"truths" are mere sets of symbols for the unknowable;
what I dream, exists for me as much as the Bank of
England or the wetness of water. I have tried to suggest

that this defence in its turn goes overfar. Some of our symbols of the hidden It behind will work, but others will not. And even in literature I have a preference—an aesthetic preference as well as a practical one—for those that do seem to me to work. A poem like Wordsworth's which praises woods as better teachers of conduct than all the sages, moves me less—other things being equal, such as style and melody—than a poem like Hardy's[1] which expresses a revulsion from this ruthless wrestle of wooden serpents for light and life, back to humanity with its kindlier loyalties. I cannot help preferring the second. And I do not want to help preferring the second. I believe its vision of phenomena is really saner and truer in the sense that it will work better in life. And I think such a preference for "truth" is a healthy instinct. I like such things; and I like to like them. (I regret all these first persons; but I speak of

[1] And yet a modern critic can write superciliously of Hardy: "His frequent psychological accuracy has almost persuaded us of his philosophical. But he thought Time mattered, for poem after poem is full of the sense that a later experience can prove an earlier experience false. The lyric tradition of our poetry was wiser; the Elizabethan poets whose ladies had been false did not burden the universe but, more correctly, their intellectual judgments with the mistake". (This is a curious dogma: there was an Elizabethan called William Shakespeare, for example, who wrote certain *Sonnets* tolerably full of invectives against both Time and the order of mundane things.) "Nor did they think their second moments more real than their first; they thought them different and less agreeable." This is, in fact, the doctrine of "emotional attitudes" carried a stage further. Now, even if one does fall under a motor-bus, it does not matter. The moment when one is reduced to jelly is no more "real" than the moment previous when one seemed safe; it is "merely different and less agreeable". This is consoling. What matter if bank-notes are forged? No "later experience can prove an earlier experience false". And the author of this fantasy taxes Hardy with being excessively "romantic"! This critic is sure that Time does not "matter"; Time is more than likely to return the compliment.

myself, as speaking only for myself, to avoid being egotistic.)

But this is perfectly compatible with admiration for a great deal of Romanticism. Much Romantic work has been mentally or emotionally dishonest; much has been, though genuine, yet morbid and hysterical. But attacks on it as "untrue" are often merely unintelligent dislike of unfamiliar symbols. Thus Rossetti jibbed at Morris's *Sigurd the Volsung* because, he said, he could not be interested in people who turned into dragons; as if we did not meet every year people who have turned or are turning into dragons, just as grimly as Fafnir brooding on his hoarded gold! If the symbol works, well and good; if the poet realizes, as Morris and Hardy did, that it is only a symbol and a dream, still better. Those who denounce all Romanticism indiscriminately are surely as extreme as if they thought algebraic equations in a, b, and c became false when stated in terms of x, y, and z. The magic potions of Tristram or Sigurd, which kindle new love or kill the old, are no less "real" or "true" than the fickle passions and infidelities of the latest novel. And if the Romantic tends to prefer symbols that are ancient, counters that are moss-grown, that is not blind caprice. Novelties may tickle the conscious curiosity; but the deeper levels are stirred by older impulses—things whose echoes go back to the childhood of the individual and the race. Modernity may bring new awakenings; but old wine and old memories bring dreams. The religious have realized that; it is not by chance that priests have still used stone knives long after the ages of bronze and iron had dawned.

Without any intellectual thimble-rigging, any striking

of emotional poses in the void, life can still be romantic
for the Romantic, poetic for the poetic; still, in Walpole's
wise phrase, "a comedy for those who think and a
tragedy for those who feel". There is still a notebook
written by Napoleon in his schooldays, of which the
closing words are "Sainte-Hélène, petite île". Fate
has not lost, with the centuries, its deadly gift of irony.

It is a question of seeing life without being hypnotized
by the superstitions of our age, with its mechanisms and
its fanaticisms; or reverting, either, to the superstitions
of the past.

> Men grow too old for love, maybe,
> Men grow too old for lies;
> But I shall not grow too old to see
> Enormous night arise;
> A cloud that is larger than the world
> And a monster made of eyes.[1]

And again—

> But now a great thing in the street
>   Seems any human nod,
> Where shift in strange democracy
>   The million masks of God.
>
> In youth I sought the golden flower
>   Hidden in wood or wold,
> But I am come to autumn
>   When all the leaves are gold.[1]

But truth is not enough without health as well. "Mens
sana in corpore sano" is not merely an ideal; it is a statement of fact. For though it is not impossible, it is not
common to find sanity incarnate in a sick frame.
Most of us learn by experience when we are depressed,
to look to our bodies, at least partly, for the cause; and

[1] G. K. Chesterton.

for the cure. Happiness is so largely a matter of mere vitality. " Mighty poets in their misery dead " has proved only too often a true saying; and mighty poets in their misery living also. The Goncourt idea of the value to a writer of being ill is not, I think, wholly false—the mind may triumph over the body—but a dangerous exaggeration. The mortifier of the flesh is merely another kind of drug-fiend. Eating too little, as the religious long since discovered, is a means to intoxication as well as drinking too much. But though sickness may bring more and vivider dreams, the dreams themselves are likely to be sick. If Greek art is perfect in its health and balance as no other art has been, that is, I believe, partly because Greek life was itself healthy and soundly balanced between body and mind, between action and thought. So with the best of the Icelandic sagas; so with Chaucer and the Ballads and Shakespeare and Ronsard. It is not to bloody revivals of Aztec gods among the aridities of Mexico or to the Nordic orgies of Nazidom, but to a happier Europe, in the first place, that it seems to me reasonable to look forward for a time when this Trinity—Classicism, Romanticism, Realism—may perhaps meet again in one—a Europe where men are bred for quality, not quantity; where the population is far smaller and less town-minded and town-hearted; where men are freed from the drudgery of mindless labour and Nature from the hideousness of industrialism. And with that new leisure it might be possible again for the mass of mankind to become in some sense creative. Creation—be it only of a hencoop—seems to me half the secret of the good life. It is the sterile, uncreative, critical or merely absorbent mind that is cursed like the barren fig-tree of Israel. The mentally passive are on their way to become mental patients. But such active originality means individualism—the very opposite of the mass-movements which are bastardizing the populations of modern Italy and Germany to a level below a healthy Polynesian. And individuality is greatly helped by a certain amount of solitude—above all by being alone with Nature, like the Wordsworth of the *Prelude*. A garden-suburb England is only too likely to produce an anaemic suburbanity. True civilization needs desert wildernesses to balance its cities.

But though it is desirable that we should think of Utopias, unless human progress is to be as blind as an Indian file of caterpillars processing round a flower-pot, it is undesirable to think too much of them. For though we may dream of our Platonic republics, it is not we who shall live in them; even if anything remotely like them ever comes to be. The individual has still to make his terms with 1936.

And even in 1936 a measured Romanticism seems to me better than that cynicism of the intellectuals of a few years back, which was often genuine, and yet not intelligent.

> Grey house and grey house and after that grey house
> Another house as grey and steep and still:
> An old cat tired of playing with a mouse,
> A sick child tired of chasing down the hill.
> Shuffle and hurry, idle feet and slow,
> Grim face and merry face, so ugly all!
> Why do you hurry? Where is there to go?
> Why are you shouting? Who is there to call?...
> If this distaste I hold for fools is such,
> Shall I not spit upon myself as well?
> Do I not eat and drink and smile as much,
> Do I not fatten also in this hell?[1]

[1] Iris Tree.

This is eloquently passionate. Yet, with such a view of the world, is the fault wholly the world's? Life was still harder and grimmer in saga Iceland; but the vitality, the zest for life were also there—a Romanticism, intensely restrained, yet real. Life was still madder in the France of Montaigne; yet that brave smiling sceptic keeps in his heart a romantic adoration for the heroes of his Plutarch. Without it he would not have kept his own heart, if one may so put it, "si gaillard et si gai". Life was still bleaker for the disillusioned old age of Hardy, with his pessimism deepened by the War and by the Peace of 1919; and yet Hardy remains to the end one of the greatest of all English romancers despite his incomparable honesty of mind.

> If I have seen one thing
> It is the passing preciousness of dreams.

It is the same with his contemporary and fellow-pessimist, the greatest classical scholar of the age; so far at first sight from *Jude the Obscure*, yet likewise a poet of pastoral England, of Shropshire as the other of Wessex—A. E. Housman. With him too beauty did not forget the bitterness of reality, but his realism did not grovel on its belly in the squalor of the dust; his Muse remains queenly as Cleopatra, while she takes the asp of Truth to her dreaming heart.

> Tell me not here, it needs not saying,
>   What tune the enchantress plays
> In aftermaths of soft September
>   Or under blanching mays,
> For she and I were long acquainted
>   And I knew all her ways.

On russet floors, by waters idle
    The pine lets fall its cone;
The cuckoo shouts all day at nothing
    In leafy dells alone;
And traveller's joy beguiles in autumn
    Hearts that have lost their own.

And so I do not understand the mentality that proclaims: "There may be a good deal to be said for
Romanticism in life, there is no place for it in letters."
It seems to me that there is certainly much to be said
for it in real life, though within reason. For it is from
a Romantic sense of life lived as tragedy, that a character
like the mother of the Bonapartes draws much of its
strength. After Waterloo, she offered her son her whole
fortune. "But you will be ruined!" "What does it
matter? When I have nothing, I will take a staff and
beg an alms for 'the mother of Napoleon'!" And again,
after the end at St Helena: "My son died miserably.
My other children are proscribed. My grandchildren
who promised best seem doomed to disappear. I am
old, forsaken, without glory, without honour—and I
would not change places with the first queen in the
world." No doubt this generous wine of dream and
pride is dangerous. It had helped her son to ruin
Europe. It is better suited to days of stress and crisis,
than of peace. It is the fuel of wars. But it is not a force
for desk-rats to despise.

Yet it is in literature, not in life, that Romanticism
seems to me, along with much rubbish, to have produced
its truest triumphs. Its immortals still man the walls of
every library in Western Europe. The Romantic Revival
may look pallid now. The Sleeping Beauty sleeps again.
She is not dead.

The Roman Empire likewise declined and fell; even to-day Italy is again in the hands of the barbarian. Yet the Roman Empire had its Eternal City. Rome will be there when its latest barbarians too have passed and silence fallen above their settling dust. So too Romance, however its flowers may wither for a season, has still its roots deep in human nature, its great trees that will long outlive ourselves. Heine's fir and palm still stand upon their everlasting hills. "Le romanesque est mort: vive le romanesque!"

CHAPTER IV

A ROMANTIC CRITIC

COLERIDGE is, in England at least, the master-critic of Romanticism; Imagination is its master-spirit; and Coleridge's theory of the Imagination, divorcing it from the Fancy, remains one of his most famous speculations. Indeed it has been treated in a recent book[1] as of vital importance to the spiritual future of the human race— a step "of the same type as that which took Galileo into the modern world". "Neither Coleridge's grounds for the distinction nor his applications of it have as yet entered our general intellectual tradition. When they do, the order of our universes will have been changed." In the face of such an impending cataclysm it may seem rash still to doubt. And yet I cannot help feeling, both here and elsewhere, that Coleridge remains an example of how much our Romantic criticism, while it gained in sensibility, tended to lose in sense.

Ancient critics were not greatly interested in the nature of Imagination, though it bothered ancient philosophers. As in mediaeval English, the creative writer was a "maker", ποιητής; and the things he made were suspect. For what difference was there between fiction and deceit? The old Solon could upbraid Thespis, the father of drama, for "getting up on a trestle and telling lies", with the same simplicity that has led modern countryfolk to abjure summer-time as falsifying

[1] Dr I. A. Richards, *Coleridge on Imagination* (1934).

the hours of God. The distinction between the imagination that reproduces past impressions and the imagination that produces new ones, was not arrived at in a day.[1]

Faced with the problem of how the first carpenter thought of the first table, Plato built up that strange and obscure system of Ideas, which enabled him to degrade the artist below the artificer, on the ground that the painter of a pictured table produced a mere secondary shadow of the carpenter's primary shadow of ideal reality—the poor imitation of an imitation.[2]

To this Aristotle replied that art was no doubt "reproduction" (*mimesis*); but so far from being a pale copy of a copy it was, on the contrary, nearer to the ideal, the general, the universal; so that the imaginative poet could claim to be more of a philosopher than the historian of actual events. It was by no mere waxwork representation, but its power to reproduce the *feelings* of real life

---

[1] It is thus misleading, I think, to say (*Coleridge on Imagination*, p. 24) that "the most ancient sense" of imagination is "imagination *contrasted* with imitation". *Imaginatio* and *imago* come, on the contrary, from the same root as *imitatio* (*ic*, *aic*: cf. εἰκών, *aequus*, *iniquus*, *aemulus*—for *aic-mulus*). *Imaginatio* means (1) the impression made by a phenomenon, as by a seal on wax; (2) the reconstruction, in the memory, of such an impression; (3) the construction, from past impressions, of some new image. Similarly the ancestor of "Fancy", the Greek φαντασία, means (1) an appearance (from the root *pha*, "light"); (2) the faculty of imagining. Thus in origin "Fancy" and "Imagination" are close cousins, with no difference in their principal meaning.

[2] The Socrates of the *Ion* does indeed offer the poetic imagination a bouquet, suggesting that it is a divine madness; and the poets of posterity have gratefully accepted it, failing to discern that there was a wasp under the flowers. The poets are no doubt "possessed", is Plato's real conclusion; but the spirit that possesses them may be good or evil, truthful or deceiving; what use, then, are poets? They are delirious dervishes, whose dreams come as easily through the Gate of Ivory as of Horn.

that music won from Aristotle the title, astonishing to us, of "most mimetic of all arts".

Another advance made by Aristotle was his recognition of the importance in literature of the power of combining images; the gift of metaphor, "of seeing likenesses", is for him a real stamp of genius, born and not made. Metaphor may seem to us only one of many arrows in the writer's quiver; authors like Swift have done almost entirely without; and it looks arbitrary to lay so much stress upon it. But it becomes less odd and arbitrary, I think, if we recall the enormous part that clinical experience has found played by symbolism and disguise in the workings of the Unconscious and of dreams.

The materialism of Democritus, Epicurus, and Lucretius was also puzzled by the Imagination. Vision and visualization, for Lucretius, are both caused by actual films, of extreme tenuity, radiated in endless succession from all bodies. We have conceptions of the gods. Therefore, said Epicurus, the gods do exist. It would have suited his general scheme far better to eliminate them. However, he could see nothing for it but to admit them and then pension them off, where they could do no harm, in "the lucid interspace of world and world". But centaurs and such chimeras he would not have. In this case we are, he said, deceived by the images of men and horses colliding and telescoping before they penetrate our minds. (No doubt when television becomes common, if the international anarchy of the ether continues, we shall be able to watch this process of Epicurus happening under our eyes; just as to-day the notes of Hitler and Haydn and jazz all unite to typify our present civilization of scientific chimpanzees.)

Why did not Epicurus explain in the same way our conception of the gods? It is hard to say. Perhaps he did not think of it. No wonder opponents like Cicero made great fun of so materialistic a theory of Imagination. And yet this idea of the amalgamation of images in the mind, obvious as it looks now, was a step in the right direction, along "the Road to Xanadu".

We should expect to find more about the artistic imagination in "Longinus", *On Great Writing* (first cent. A.D.?). But that author contents himself with saying that "the first and foremost thing in great literature is the power of forming great conceptions"—things independent of the words they are written in, like the silence of Ajax in Hades; and, again, that such literary greatness is "the echo of a great personality". Too much, again, has been made of a passage in Philostratus (third cent. A.D.), where Apollonius of Tyana, that ancient Paracelsus, discusses Imagination (φαντασία) with the naked sages he visited in Egypt (VI, 19). The Greek finds fault with the beast-gods of Egypt by contrast with the superhuman Zeus of Phidias or Aphrodite of Praxiteles. "How did your artists know what the gods were like?" sneers a nettled Egyptian. "By going and seeing them in Heaven?" "It was Imagination," replies Apollonius, "a more cunning artist than Imitation. For Imitation can only fashion what it has seen, but Imagination what it has not seen, also; conceiving it on the analogy of what exists (ὑποθήσεται γὰρ αὐτὸ πρὸς τὴν ἀναφορὰν τοῦ ὄντος)."[1]

---

[1] The version of Mr E. F. Carritt in his *Philosophies of Beauty*— "imagination goes on to what it has not seen, which it will assume as the standard of the reality"—seems to me completely out of relation to the Greek; similarly his rendering of τέχνη in Plotinus, V, 8, 1. The word

But it hardly needed a prophet to tell us this. The Muses had already made this distinction, in essence, between the productive and the reproductive imagination, when they met Hesiod on Helicon a thousand years before, singing

> Many things false our lips like truth can utter,
> But true things, too, at will our tongues can tell.

The fact is, I think, that the Greeks with their strong "reality-principle" were less interested in Imagination than later generations with their craving for new inventions in a staler world and for wish-fulfilling dreams in a tormented one. Thus Greek poetry and drama were largely content with lovely variations of that imaginative mythology whose origins were lost even for them; their best prose concentrated not on fiction, but on oratory, history, and philosophy; and we have seen how they distrusted the fantastic and far-fetched—an incident like men turning into swine, or even a metaphor like "holding the mirror up to life". The Greek mind, when serious, was usually sober. For wilder flights we must look to Aristophanes, whose Muse of Comedy was a younger daughter, licensed in extravagance; to Plato, who is untypical; to Lucian and the novelists, who are late.

In English criticism Imagination and Fancy long remained the same; in Puttenham, who writes indifferently of "disordered phantasies" and "monstrous imaginations"; in Shakespeare, for whom Antony is "Nature's piece 'gainst fancy" (just as his Cleopatra

---

means simply "knowledge of his art", and might apply equally to a cobbler. The art in this case does involve imagination; but that is another matter. Like later Platonists, Plotinus here adds little to his master.

correspondingly recalls a picture where "we see the fancy outwork Nature"), while

> The lunatic, the lover, and the poet
> Are of imagination all compact;

in Sir William Temple, who speaks of "imagination or fancy"; in Addison, who strangely supposes both alike to be based entirely on past *visual* impressions. But a distinction does appear in Dryden's Preface to *Annus Mirabilis*, where he divides Wit or Imagination into Invention, which invents; Fancy, which varies and arranges these materials provided by Invention; and Elocution, which moulds the style.

But Dryden's idea of Fancy as a part of Imagination does not seem to have had much success. The two words lived on side by side; with a tendency, I think, for Fancy, helped by its sister-words "fantasy" and "fantastic", by its other meanings, like "love", and perhaps by its very sound, to seem the weaker vessel, the more frivolous, capricious and feminine of the two.

Then came Coleridge, to put them firmly asunder. "Imagination I consider either as primary, or secondary. The primary Imagination I hold to be the living power and primary agent of all human perception, and as a repetition in the finite mind of the eternal act of creation in the infinite I AM. The secondary Imagination I consider as an echo of the former, co-existing with the conscious will, yet still as identical with the primary in the *kind* of its agency, and differing only in *degree*, and in the mode of its operation. It dissolves, diffuses, dissipates in order to recreate: or where this process is rendered impossible, yet still at all events it struggles to idealize and to unify. It is essentially vital, even as all objects (*as* objects) are essentially fixed and dead.

FANCY, on the contrary, has no other counters to play with but fixities and definites. The fancy is indeed no other than a mode of memory emancipated from the order of time and space."[1]

Perhaps it would not be unfair to illustrate this obscure and contorted statement as follows. Imagine human minds as equipped with radio and television sets. The Infinite I AM transmits; the primary imagination[2] within us reproduces that shadow-show we call "Reality". God creates; we re-create. He conceives; we perceive.

The secondary imagination, on the other hand—what we usually call "imagination" simply—can stage similar dream-dramas in its own studio. Like a lesser deity, the poetic mind says "Let there be delight"; and there is delight.

Fancy, on the other hand, can only make patchwork screens—*collages*—with fixed photographs from the store of memory. It can combine new patterns; but it works with "fixities and definites".[3]

It is like the difference, we might say, between the novelist who creates a Don Quixote or an Uncle Toby and the novelist who fits into his story "portraits" of his

[1] *Biog. Lit.* XIII.
[2] It will be seen that this use of "imagination" for our power of *apprehending* the universe about us is a highly unusual one which helps, I think, to cause confusion when we pass on to imagination in the ordinary sense.
[3] Coleridge seems to exaggerate, when he talks as if any mental impressions could really retain this fixity, like stones of a mosaic; they are rather wisps of cloud, perpetually reshaped by the shifting winds of the Unconscious.

acquaintances: between the writer who builds a complete new world of his own, like Dickens, and the writer who merely reshuffles autobiographical experiences.

Elsewhere Coleridge calls Imagination the "Esemplastic Power", because it produces new unities.[1] It is "the greatest faculty of the human mind". It is "the power by which one image or feeling is made to modify many others, and by a sort of fusion to force many into one"; the power "of combining many circumstances into one moment of thought to produce that ultimate end of human thought and human feeling, unity, and thereby the reduction of the spirit to its principle and fountain, who is alone truly *One*".

Now with theories of the universe at large we are not here concerned. This idea that the "ultimate end of all human thought and human feeling" is "unity" may be the profoundest of truths or it may be mere homesickness for the womb—that is not here the question: the only point at issue is—does Coleridge's distinction work with literature?

Leaving on one side, then, the reduction of the spirit

[1] It is perhaps typical of Coleridge's absences of taste that he should coin such a horror; and of his absences of mind that the coinage should be false at that. "Esemplastic", could it exist, would mean "into-*in*-moulding", not "into-*one*-moulding". Elsewhere he makes the necessary correction to "es-eno-plastic"; but mends his Greek only to flounder in German: "How excellently the German *Einbildungskraft* (power in imagination) expresses this prime and loftiest faculty—In-eins-bildung!" Needless to say the "Ein-" means "into", not "one": "sich einbilden" = "to introduce an image into one's own mind". One is reminded of his amazing statement that "Epic" comes from "ἕπομαι, *sequor*" (instead of ἕπος, "word", "speech", "tale"), in support of his highly questionable distinction between Epic and Drama. These pedantries are little in themselves: but they are symptomatic, I think, of the way the clutch is apt to slip in Coleridge's mind (cf. his famous misuse of ἕστησε).

to its fountain, whatever that may mean, let us turn to his few examples—all too few—of the literary Imagination.[1] Its working may be:

A. Passionate. As when Lear "spreads the feeling of ingratitude and cruelty over the very elements of Heaven"; or the Shakespeare of the *Sonnets* says of his indifference to all the birds and flowers of spring in his love's absence—

> As with your shadow, I with these did play.

Or B. Tranquil. Here Imagination may unify in two ways:

(1) It seems to reduce a multitude of phenomena to one, as "when we open our eyes upon an extended prospect" from a hilltop; or a number of successive events to an instant, as when Adonis leaves Venus:

> Look! how a bright star shooteth from the sky,
> So glides he in the night from Venus' eye.

Or (2) When it impresses the stamp of human feelings on non-human objects:

> Lo! here the gentle lark, weary of rest,
> From his moist cabinet mounts up on high.[2]

We have here, in fact, a new Three Unities—in passion, in extension or duration, and in humanization. They make a queer trio.

Fancy, on the other hand, assembles her images, it appears, like a bower-bird collecting objects bright or odd; and arranges them, unchanged in themselves, about her door. Or, to change the illustration, she makes

---

[1] See T. M. Raysor, *Coleridge's Shakespearean Criticism*, 1, 212 ff., *Biog. Lit.* xv.

[2] This seems merely a calmer repetition of A. In either case natural objects are *humanized*.

barren marriages of ideas, which do not, like those blessed by Imagination, produce a new creation. Or again, one might say, Fancy produces a physical mixture, as of sulphur and iron filings, where either element remains intact; whereas the heat of Imagination creates a new compound, like iron sulphide, which this time no magnet can separate.

This theory of Imagination and Fancy as quite different things has been a good deal criticized—by Walter Pater, by Professor Lascelles Abercrombie, by Professor Livingston Lowes. And they in their turn have been severely reproved by Dr Richards, who likens their utterances to those of a schoolboy or "a Schoolmaster's Report". "Pater's is amateur's work, mere nugatory verbiage—empty, rootless and backgroundless postulation—unless we put into it just that very piece of patient laborious analysis that it pretends so airily to dismiss and surpass." To which Pater might have gently murmured that perhaps the "verbiage" was not altogether on one side.

But it remains to test, even at the risk of excommunication, how far this theory will really work in practice. Thus as an example of Fancy Coleridge quotes from *Venus and Adonis*:[1]

> Full gently now she takes him by the hand,
> A lily prisoned in a jail of snow,
> Or ivory in an alabaster band;
> So white a friend engirts so white a foe.

These similes, he says, bring together objects "dissimilar in the main, by some one point or more of likeness distinguished". Adonis' hand is white; so is a lily or

[1] Raysor, I, 212–13.

ivory. Venus' hand is white; so is snow or alabaster.
And Venus' hand imprisons her love's as a jail imprisons
a prisoner.

But even at this point discrepancies already begin to
arise. For Dr Richards the last line is an example, not
of Fancy, but of Imagination. For Venus' hand is
a friend in *two* senses: (*a*) she loves Adonis; (*b*) she would
have saved his life, had he listened and not gone hunting.
This double sense produces, for Dr Richards, "consiliences and reverberations".[1] Coleridge, on the other
hand, allowed Fancy "one point *or more* of likeness";
and quotes the whole passage as fanciful. Which is right?
Can we honestly detect quite a different activity of mind
in this fourth line from that at work in the other three?

On the other hand this, we are told, is a case of
Imagination:

> Look! how a bright star shooteth from the sky,
> So glides he in the night from Venus' eye.

Here, says Coleridge, are combined a number of images
and feelings—the beauty of Adonis, the rapidity of his
flight, the yearning helplessness of Venus. And Dr
Richards discovers a whole host of other "links of
relevance"—Venus is like the night in being darkened
by her sense of loss; Adonis is like the star in being
a giver of light, an influence, "a destiny"; the sky, but
now a source of light, has become a source of ruin; and
so forth.

To some readers this will seem a highly fanciful
picture of Imagination. Is this idea of the astrological
influence of stars really relevant? Or is it a piece of

[1] *Coleridge on Imagination*, p. 84.

"metaphysical" ingenuity, confounding the beauty of simplicity by its covetousness? Personally, I find the lines call up two simple visual images in succession—a starry sky whence falls a meteor; and then the young Adonis vanishing in the shadows. To cram in references to horoscopes and the like seems to me like spoiling the reflection of that starlit heaven in a quiet lake by pitching pebbles into it. I recognize that there are "nine and sixty ways" of reading, as well as of writing, "tribal lays": but I am not tempted to change in the hope of more "consiliences and reverberations"—

> Curling with metaphors a plain intention,
> Decking the sense, as if it were to sell.

When Cyrus the Persian felt insulted by the River Gyndes because it had drowned one of his sacred white horses, he swore to break its pride and wasted a whole campaign splitting it into three hundred and sixty channels, till a woman could cross without wetting her knee; many modern minds seem to think they honour the great streams of poetry by a similar process.

Contrast this other starlit scene from Homer, as rendered by Tennyson:

> As when in heaven the stars about the moon
> Look beautiful, when all the winds are laid,
> And every height comes out, and jutting peak
> And valley, and the immeasurable heavens
> Break open to their highest, and all the stars
> Shine, and the Shepherd gladdens in his heart;
> So many a fire between the ships and stream
> Of Xanthus blazed.

Here the only point of likeness is that between many twinkling fires and many twinkling stars; the rest, as so often in Homeric similes, is a divine bounty, little tied by "links of relevance". Is this, then, a case of Fancy, not Imagination? The work of a lower faculty? For myself, I would always have given the whole of *Venus and Adonis*, except its hunted hare and its dive-dapper and its snail, for these few lines; even before I came to see how magnificent is Homer's contrast between the lurid darkness of the battlefield and that happy Wordsworthian shepherd on his moonlit fells.

Homer cares so little in general for "cross-connections" that he will compare the Trojans' clamour as they march to meet the Greeks to the windy cry of the cranes flying south to fight the pygmies; without fearing lest some too ingenious Achaean should upbraid him for suggesting that the Greek heroes in the least resembled pygmies. Or take that terrible vision of Beddoes, where pestilence-stricken air becomes

> Transparent as the glass of poisoned water
> Through which the drinker sees his murderer smiling.

Poisoned transparent air—poisoned transparent water—there do not seem many "links of relevance"; and yet the lines would seem to me "imaginative" even if I did not even know what the water was supposed to resemble. Who cares, again, in the great simile at the end of Arnold's *Scholar-Gipsy*, that the things compared are so "dissimilar in the main"? The *care-free* Scholar is bidden by Arnold to shun the *melancholy* modern thinker, as the *grave* Phoenician turned away from the *merry* Grecian trader out into the wild Atlantic. The "links of relevance" are thin indeed; yet are we to deny the passage Imagination?

Or consider a couplet that most would class, if they had to choose, as "Fancy":

> Words are like leaves and, where they most abound,
> Much fruit of sense beneath is rarely found.

If one likes this game of hunting for "cross-connection after cross-connection", these lines of Pope provide admirable opportunities.

Leaves are like words because:

(1) By their abundance they use up the energy which should have borne fruit.

(2) In large numbers, they obscure.

(3) They grow old and decay.

(4) They are made audible by the wind, as words by breath. They have even formed sentences, as at Dodona.

(5) They can be printed.

Fruit is like sense, because:

(1) It nourishes.

(2) It matures slowly.

(3) It is itself fruitful, and able to propagate.

(4) It is often hard to reach.

This sort of game of seeing analogies can be pursued indefinitely; does it make the passage an example of Imagination—except in the critic?

At this point I must add there seems to me a certain divergence between Coleridge and his modern interpreter. For Coleridge what mattered was the emotional *unity* that Imagination produced from multiplicity, as moonlight, he said, transfigures a whole landscape; Dr Richards, I suspect, is much more delighted intellectually by the *multiplicity* out of which that unity is produced. I doubt if Coleridge would have shared all this enthusiasm for ambiguities and "numbers of connections", or felt reassured by being told they need not be consciously noted. Coleridge, in other words, is pleased by the process which can reduce so many odd pence to a single pound; his commentator by counting over how many pence that pound contains. Dr Richards, indeed, frankly admits that he is not altogether sure nor much interested how far Coleridge would have accepted all that he has built on Coleridge's foundations. Indeed it seems natural enough that there should be a good deal of discrepancy between the pious ancestor of the Oxford Movement and this interpreter whose "Benthamite materialism", however mingled with mysticism, would have filled Coleridge with horror and consternation. *Coleridge on Imagination* contains, I feel, a certain amount of imagination on Coleridge.[1]

To return, Coleridge produces certain further illustrations of his contrast between Imagination and Fancy.[2]

> Behold yon row of pines, that shorn and bow'd
> Bend from the sea-blast, seen at twilight eve.

"When a human and intellectual life is transferred to them from the poet's own spirit", he says, these lines

---

[1] It should be remembered that his main discussions of Fancy and Imagination in *Biographia Literaria* (1815–17) and the Lectures of 1818 were written when Coleridge had become devoutly Christian; and are much later than the passage in *The Aeolian Harp* (1795) and the letter to Thelwall in 1796 which lie nearer to the philosophy of Dr Richards. Of course one can always say "Coleridge was *not* a Christian, if he had only known"; but there remains a constant danger of muddle, when one sets out to understand the dead so much better than they understood themselves. "Il y a des esprits qui ne peuvent admettre et admirer les autres qu'en les tirant à soi."   [2] *Biog. Lit.* xv.

become imaginative and "rise into semblance of poetry":

> Yon row of bleak and visionary pines,
> By twilight glimpse discerned, mark! how they flee
> From the fierce sea-blast, all their tresses wild
> Streaming before them.

Corrupted by a classical education, I find myself perversely giving the preference, if any, to the quieter tone of the first passage. In the second, the trees have become "bleak and visionary", they are "by glimpse discerned" instead of "seen", and in addition we are adjured to "mark" them; but does one mark them more highly for protesting so much more?[1] If it is so imaginative to "humanize" objects, the trees in the first passage were already "shorn and bowed", as if they were men, or at least animals. Do their new "tresses" really add so much? Is this sort of poetic anthropomorphism necessarily so imaginative? Are we then to admire for its imagination the winter of Sylvester's Du Bartas, which comes

> To glaze the Lake, to bridle up the Floods,
> And periwig with snow the bald-pate Woods?

Surely this is, if anything, "fanciful"; just as Coleridge classes Cowley as "fanciful", in contrast to Milton who is "imaginative". Take, on the other hand, Housman's

> Fall, winter, fall; for he,
> Prompt hand and headpiece clever,
> Has woven a winter-robe,
> And made of earth and sea
> His overcoat for ever
> And wears the turning globe.

---

[1] Incidentally, it is not clear that the second version has acquired many more "cross-connections" or "links of relevance" or "supernumerary meanings".

Is this not "imaginative", as well as fanciful? Yet what "cross-connections", what "links of relevance" are there between "earth and *sea*" and an overcoat, except that the buried feel no more cold?[1]

Or again consider Wordsworth's example of the contrast:

> The dews of the evening most carefully shun,
> They are the tears of the sky for the loss of the sun.
> (Chesterfield.)

> Sky lowered, and, muttering thunder, some sad drops
> Wept at completion of the mortal sin.   (Milton.)

The comparison is equally simple in either case; the sky weeps for the sun, or for the sin; are there more "consiliences and reverberations" in one passage than the other? Is the enormous difference between them a matter of (poetic phrase!) "secondary and tertiary co-implications among their possibilities of interpretation"?

And, after all, why this constant preoccupation with similes and metaphors? One would think Imagination consisted chiefly in implying A is like B in $n + 1$ ways. For a companion-piece to Adonis' parting from Venus, as "a bright star shooteth from the sky", which is supposed to be so vastly imaginative, turn to Achilles' parting from Odysseus among the dead, consoled for a moment in his deathless melancholy by hearing of the brave deeds of his son on earth:

> ψυχὴ δὲ ποδώκεος Αἰακίδαο
> φοίτα μακρὰ βιβῶσα κατ' ἀσφοδελὸν λειμῶνα.

> But the soul of swift Aeacides
> With mighty strides went stalking down the mead of asphodel.

---

[1] I imagine that Coleridge might have agreed. The stanza has an emotional unity, though again few "supernumerary meanings".

A mightier than Adonis is here, leaning in his giant simplicity on no "cross-references". Or recall the episode of the death of the dog Argus, after he has laid back his ears and twitched his tail at the sight of the master whose nearest and dearest failed to know him in his rags.

> Ἄργον δ' αὖ κατὰ μοῖρ' ἔλαβεν μέλανος θανάτοιο,
> αὐτίκ' ἰδόντ' Ὀδυσῆα ἐεικοστῷ ἐνιαυτῷ.

But the doom of death's long darkness on Argus fell at last
The day he had seen Odysseus, when the twentieth year
was past.

The dog Argus, covered with lice on his dunghill, has outlived a hundred generations of men. Why? Because he was so complex? No, because he was so simple—with the simplicity of the eternal sorrows of our dust. And that is why he will be remembered three thousand years hence, long after our paper flowers of criticism have gone the forgotten way of better things. When Coleridge pronounced that there was "nothing sublime" in Greek, he might perhaps have been better employed in learning a little more of it.

The truth is, I think, that he pursued Unity everywhere, with the eagerness of Sir Thomas Browne pursuing Quincunces, because of its mystical connection in his mind with the Unity of God and unity with God;[1]

---

[1] How strong this strange craving for unity was in Coleridge comes out clearly in a letter to Thelwall in 1797 (quoted in J. Shawcross's edition of the *Biographia Literaria*, i, xviii): "The universe itself, what but an immense heap of little things?... My mind feels as if it ached to behold and know something *great*, something *one* and *indivisible*. And it is only in the faith of that, that rocks or waterfalls, mountains or caverns, give me the sense of sublimity or majesty! But in this faith *all things* counterfeit infinity." To minds without this mystical yearning it seems

while Dr Richards, regarding all our views of the universe as alike mythological, feels that the more there are, and the more complex, the merrier.

But transcendental mysticism may not be altogether helpful in building critical theories. In critical practice the ensuing theories may lead to that fatal mistake of laying down rules and judging by them. And yet perhaps the only rule in criticism is that we should never criticize by rules. "The poet", Coleridge tells us, "should paint to the imagination, not to the fancy." For Coleridge's disciple, indeed, the Imagination is no longer in itself of greater value than the Fancy; only of wider range. None the less, this notion of the surpassing preciousness of "consiliences and reverberations" leads on to a condemnation of Rupert Brooke's poetry, as contrasted with Mr Auden's or Mr Empson's, on the ground that "it has no *inside*. Its ideas and other components, however varied, are all expressed with prominence...." (How horrible! All the brutal lucidity of a Sappho or a Horace, a Herrick or a Racine!) "The

as strange to want the whole universe to have one essence as to want it to have only one colour—say, bright pink.

It is no doubt possible to believe that the world about us is the Book of God, in which all phenomena are but symbols of Him; the Fancy playing with those symbols as a child that cannot read, the Imagination reading them as wholes by which in moments of vision it communicates with Him. It is possible to believe it: but why should one? Because of the wish to; and if one has not the faintest wish?

I believe, though it cannot be proved, that this mystic eagerness for unity is due ultimately to a loss of nerve. As man has grown more individual and intelligent, he has grown more divided and solitary. Men are not lemmings—   Alone the sun arises, and alone
                Spring the great streams.

But at moments, realizing that "nous sommes irrémédiablement seuls", the mind grows sick and giddy and runs for refuge to the mystic's trance— or the totalitarian state.

reader is visiting an Exhibition of Poetic Products."
It would be simple to reply that one may prefer that to
an Exhibition of Raw Materials. But in judging poets
arguments settle little or nothing. It is enough to point
out what an enormous amount of the world's poetry,
especially Greek and French, such an attitude brands
as inferior with a firmness that recalls Dr Richards's
observation that "the greater part of Greek tragedy as
well as almost all Elizabethan Tragedy outside Shakespeare's six masterpieces" is "pseudo-tragedy". Is such
exclusiveness not in danger of growing, perhaps, a little
extreme? His *Practical Criticism* showed, I feel, a wiser
uncertainty.

It still seems to me, then, unnecessary to assume two
perfectly distinct "faculties", Fancy and Imagination.
On the other hand the two words have now acquired a
definite difference in common speech. Can we analyse
our spontaneous use of them? What makes us call one
thing "fanciful", another "imaginative"? I believe
that the difference we feel lies rather in the *way* the writer
applies his gifts of style and imagery—not in the powers
he employs so much as in the tone and intention with
which he employs them. He can use language mainly
to communicate his own feelings; or mainly to excite
feelings in his audience—feelings largely of admiration
or astonishment at his style and ingenuity. Thus Lord
Chesterfield exhibits a clever *conceit* about dew which will
cause a neat click in his reader's mind; but Milton is
striving to share with us his *conception* of the horror which
oppressed the universe at sight of that first fatal dis-
obedience. Chesterfield's eye is focussed on his own wit;
Milton's on the horror of man's sin and God's wrath.

In fine, you may use language in two ways, as you may use glass to make a window through which others shall see the landscape of your vision; or to make a stained-glass window, which will not so much give light, or sight of something beyond, as pleasure by its own colour and pattern. You may stretch the golden wire of words to transmit a deeply felt message; or twist it into some elaborate bangle. But of course the two usages are not mutually exclusive; and there are infinite gradations. Good Metaphysical poetry, like Marvell's *Coy Mistress*, does both; bad Metaphysical poetry, like parts of his *Nunappleton House*, where distant cattle in a meadow are likened to fleas or pimples on a face, does not communicate the poet's love of the landscape, but merely his love of playing with childish "cross-connections". Dryden, before he had fully exchanged the Metaphysical follies of his youth for that gentlemanly wit which Pope was to perfect, could say of a sea-fight:

> The Foe approach'd, and one, for his bold Sin,
> Was sunk (as he that touch'd the Ark was slain:)
> The wild Waves master'd him and suck'd him in,
> And smiling *Eddies* dimpled on the Main.

Here Dryden is not concerned, like Tennyson in *The Revenge*, to fill us with the anguish and suspense and pity of a real sea-fight; he is out to draw ingenious parallels meeting only at infinity; to find likenesses between "things dissimilar in the main", that shall be precious for their very unlikeliness, as strawberries in December. Here the Foe is not really "sinning"; the English ship is not really holy; the very eddies "dimple", because the whole thing is a sham fight and a regatta. The poet is not using his wings to fly with, but to feather shuttlecocks. With this fanciful passage of Dryden Dr Richards has contrasted, as Imagination, the couplet of Sir John Beaumont:

> Here are sands, ignoble things,
> Dropt from the ruin'd sides of kings.

But here too the essential difference seems to me that the poet is trying seriously to *share* his own feelings at Westminster; till in his awed hearer there rise responsively old memories of mouldering graveyards and *Hic jacets*, memories reaching back to childhood and half lost in the mists of the Unconscious. And the sense of Unity harped on by Coleridge does tend to show itself in this kind of poetry, *because* the poet is thus sharing his own mood, bidding us gaze through his window into his world; and in so far as his state of mind at the moment and his personality in general may be expected to show a certain unity, as a magnet patterns iron filings along its lines of force, we may well feel something of that unity. We are entering into communion, not with God, but with a poet. But neither as a reader nor a writer of poetry can I by any introspection find anything more than this; though of course this may be merely my own blindness.

> Tell me where is Fancy[1] bred,
> Or in the heart, or in the head?

The answer seems—"In the head"; whereas with Imagination, the heart is involved also. The writer who would make us call him "imaginative", who would produce Macbeths as well as Queen Mabs, must have not only intellectual gifts, but also a personality great enough, as "Longinus" meant, to echo through his

[1] In the original context, of course, Fancy is simply "love".

style; a personality great enough to forget its audience,
and often itself also, in its subject; so that, growing
unselfconscious, it can draw far more freely on those
stores of the Unconscious which the eighteenth century
kept so over-disciplined.[1] This, I think, is partly why
the poetry of that period in particular tends to seem much
more fanciful than imaginative.

Thus Prospero (the contrast was made by Leslie
Stephen) threatens Ariel that he will

rend an oak
And peg thee in his knotty entrails, until
Thou hast howled away twelve winters.

And every hearer at the Globe felt as if he were himself
being squeezed in that oaken vice. But the reader is
merely delighted by the dainty ingenuity with which the
Sylphs of Pope

Be stuff'd in vials, or transfix'd with pins,
Or plung'd in lakes of bitter washes lie,
Or wedg'd whole ages in a bodkin's eye.

Here the poet is not going to the bottom of the situation,
he is gaily figure-skating on its polished, frozen surface.
He is self-possessed; not possessed. Not that Imagination,
either, was lacking to the writer who could describe, for
example, with the sting of Tacitus, ladies of fashion in
their fading years—

Still round and round the ghosts of Beauty glide
And haunt the places where their honour died.

[1] Cf. J. Renard, *Journal*, 291 (the actress Moreno's account of her state
of mind): "Non, dit-elle! Un acteur n'est jamais dans la peau de son
héros, mais il n'est plus dans la sienne. Quand je joue Monime, je ne
pense pas à Monime, mais je ne suis plus Moreno. Je suis métamorphosée
en je ne sais quoi de vibrant, de surexcité, d'embêté. Je suis un être qui
a le trac, qui est en coton, et qui sue".

In a word, Coleridge seems to me to cut himself with William of Occam's razor—*entia non sunt multiplicanda*—in calling on two different faculties to explain this difference that we all feel. Donne or Marvell provides an excellent example of how one and the same gift of words and imagery can be used to produce results now magnificent, now maundering. But I doubt if a distinction often so debatable and terms so hazy can in any case be of much practical use. Coleridge's whole theory seems to me an example of that barren type of classification so dear to those who believe that if they can invent a few transcendental pigeon-holes, the Holy Spirit of poetry will descend to nest in them.[1]

The same Germanic fondness for general principles marks also Coleridge's famous dispute with Wordsworth on Poetic Diction. Gray, it will be recalled, had said, surely with extreme rashness, "the language of the age is never the language of poetry". Piqued by the cold reception of *Lyrical Ballads*, Wordsworth sat down in 1800 to write a Preface. He began with a reasonable defence of simplicity against the tinsel of poetic conven-

---

[1] For example, Ruskin, being a brave and honest critic, whether one agrees with him or not, is not afraid to be absolutely explicit when he handles the question (*Modern Painters* (1888), vol. II, pt. III, sect. II).

"Bring the rathe primrose, that forsaken dies,	*Imagination.*
The tufted crow-toe and pale jessamine,	*Nugatory.*
The white pink, and the pansy freaked with jet,	*Fancy.*
The glowing violet,	*Fancy.*
The musk rose and the well-attired woodbine,	*Vulgar.*
With cowslips wan that hang the pensive head,	*Imagination.*
And every flower that sad embroidery wears.	*Mixed.*"

This is at least clear. But is it very convincing (except for that "*Mixed*")? And is it very helpful?

tion; but his pen grew more and more violent as it progressed. "There neither is, nor can be," (how *could* he thus sit down to legislate for the future also?) "any *essential* difference between the language of prose and metrical composition." "In works of imagination and sentiment...in proportion as ideas and feelings are valuable, whether the composition be in prose or verse, they require and exact one and the same language." The poet "to excite rational sympathy must express himself as other men express themselves".[1] "There are few persons of good sense who would not allow that the dramatic parts of composition are defective in proportion as they deviate from the real language of nature[2] and are coloured by a diction of the Poet's own." And yet, one murmurs,

> To lie in cold obstruction, and to rot....

> The multitudinous Seas incarnadine....

> Looke where he comes: Not Poppy, nor Mandragora,
> Nor all the drowsie Syrrups of the world....

> Let such bethink them, if the sleepy drench
> Of that forgetful Lake benumme not still....

Each time the wonder grows what "sleepy drench" could make Wordsworth come to this. Finally, he concludes, where he should have begun, with an Appendix, far from accurate, on the practice of poets in the past. Indeed, his actual evidence throughout is limited to

---

[1] This surely disposes of any notion that by "language" Wordsworth meant merely "vocabulary"—which would indeed be a very strange use of language.

[2] In the later version of his Preface Wordsworth makes more prominent the idea that the poet's style should be "a *selection*" of common speech. This is much more reasonable, clearly, though still too narrow.

a mediocre sonnet by Gray, from which he draws
conclusions that do not follow; a stanza of the *Babes in
the Wood*; and two pieces by Johnson and by Cowper,
who is found guilty of "vicious" writing because he says
the valleys of Selkirk's island

> Ne'er sighed at the sound of a knell
> Or smiled when a Sabbath appeared.

Seventeen years later, in *Biographia Literaria* (1817),
Coleridge replied.[1] He begins with a long disquisition
maintaining that poetry, even of the highest kind, need
not be in metre;[2] argues that Wordsworth's most interesting characters are not "rustics",[3] with a digression
on the administration of the Poor Law in Liverpool as
contrasted with agricultural districts; shows that the
language of rustics is largely derived from the educated
classes (to which Wordsworth could easily have retorted
that he was not concerned with what it was derived from,
but what it *was*); and at length makes a real point, that
Wordsworth's own style is not that of rustics, particularly
in the *order* of its words. Then we are told that the metre
of poetry is created by the effort to curb excitement (which
seems doubtful) and yet creates excitement;[4] therefore

[1] *Biog. Lit.* XVII–XXII.

[2] Which does not prevent him from stating a few chapters later (XVIII)
that "poetry is imperfect and defective without metre".

[3] Wordsworth is not as clear as he might be; but he appears to mean
(1) that poets should in general use the speech of "men in real life";
and (2) that of all men in real life rustics are the sincerest in feeling, the
plainest and most emphatic in speech. Still it seems a little captious of
Coleridge to deny the name of "rustic" to an old shepherd like Wordsworth's Michael.

[4] Metre, like the beating of a tom-tom, seems actually to be a means
of exciting yet hypnotizing the hearer, so that he is both spell-bound like
the Mariner's Wedding-guest and at the same time more suggestible
to whatever he is told.

the language of poetry *must* be excited and exciting also. "I write in metre because I am about to use a language different from that of prose." "Where the language is not such...the metre *must* often become feeble." But surely this proves too much. What, we may ask, are there not passages in Chaucer and Dryden and Landor and Christina Rossetti that practise Wordsworth's theory of diction better than he did himself, keeping even the *order*[1] of prose, without the metre becoming in the least "feeble"?

> Proud word you never spoke, but you will speak
> Four not exempt from pride some future day,
> Resting on one white hand a warm wet cheek
> Over my open volume you will say
> "This man loved me", then rise and trip away.[2]

Is this "a language different from that of prose"? Is the metre "feeble"?

> What dost thinke on?—
> Nothing; of nothing: leave thy idle questions,
> I am ith way to study a long silence.
> To prate were idle, I remember nothing.
> Thers nothing of so infinit vexation
> As mans owne thoughts.[3]

Is this "a language different from that of prose"? Is the metre "feeble"? Had Coleridge never read any French poetry? But no, the only French book he could "tolerate" was a comic poem on a parrot, Gresset's *Vert-vert*.[4] (What an avowal for a critic!) However, a few pages later he calmly admits that there exists poetry, as in Chaucer and Herbert, "so worded that the reader

---

[1] Except for a moment, when speaking of *The Babes in the Wood*, Wordsworth had quite ignored the order of words, though it is hardly less important than the choice of them, in producing remoteness from common speech. [2] Landor. [3] Webster. [4] Raysor, II, 39.

sees no one reason, either in the selection or the order of the words, why he might not have said the very same in an appropriate conversation". But what then becomes of his previous statements? He had forgotten them?

But with Coleridge as with Wordsworth it is only at the end (after some fifty pages) that he makes that appeal to actual practice which could alone settle the point. Even then he is content with answering Wordsworth on Gray's Sonnet and quoting a few other scraps of English verse, quite inadequate in range.

Surely any scientist of literary interests, faced with the problem, would have immediately put out his hand to the bookshelf and discovered what is pleasing in poetry by systematically examining what has in fact pleased. A few minutes with a lexicon and a grammar would have shown him that Greek contains hundreds of words, verbal forms, and constructions found in verse alone and not in prose; similarly, to a smaller extent, with Latin. He would have found that Homer's language was a mixture of dialects, never spoken anywhere; that Dante thought a similarly eclectic language right for Italian poetry. Spenser, Shakespeare and the Elizabethans, Milton and Herrick, Dryden and the Augustans, would have further shown that English poets have succeeded both with poetic diction and without, though mostly with. And *then* he could have summed up his conclusions in an afternoon and a couple of pages. Indeed, it might suffice, for answering Wordsworth, to ask oneself whether "The Ancient Mariner" could be rechristened, without loss, "The Old Sailor". It is surely clear that "poetic diction" is not always bad nor yet essential; without it poetry is still possible, but as a whole would be immensely poorer.

All this evidence was known to Coleridge; it was decisive; it should surely have come first. But both combatants have an instinctive preference for arguing from "general principles", in a way which recalls Dante's arguments that Adam *must* have spoken first and not, as the Bible reports, "that most presumptuous Eve"; that he *must* have spoken before being spoken to; that he *must* have spoken to God; that he *must* have spoken Hebrew; that he *must* have said "El". It was thus, too, that Sir Thomas Browne pondered whether badgers' legs are longer on one side or not, by considering if it were "an affront unto Reason and generally repugnant unto the course of Nature"; with arguments adduced from frogs, spiders, beetles, grasshoppers, lobsters, and locusts. It would surely be rather simpler to examine a number of badgers—or of poets. Yet such is the general level, in English criticism, of reasoning from evidence, that this controversy between Wordsworth and Coleridge is celebrated to this day by leading critics as "the most magnificent piece of critical writing in the English language" or "one of the very *apices* of English criticism"; while Saintsbury (who has, on the other hand, little use for distinctions between Fancy and Imagination) calls Coleridge's share in it "his capital critical achievement" and "one of the patterns of a critical study".

The best poetry of Coleridge remains beyond reproach, and almost beyond praise; though he was also uncritical enough to print some of the poorest doggerel in the language. Even if one were cold to *The Ancient Mariner*, it would be foolish to attack poetry that has proved for a century its "strange power of speech". But in criticism, in so far as it is a matter of reasoning, there can be no such sacred immunity. The whole subject is far too beset with cant. And it seems to me a poor service to the young, especially, to hold up these pages of rambling as a masterpiece of hard thought. Every year the fruits of such mental vagueness show themselves in the contrast between most of the literary and scientific dissertations that I see. Only too often the literary theorists have no idea of what justifies a generalization; looking for evidence, or thinking, would break their flow of language; and yet frequently, in their desire to say everything with flowers, they do not even write so well as the scientists. Where a biologist spends days and nights counting the whiskers of hundreds of caterpillars before making a single induction, your literary critic will glance at three instances and leap. On this very matter of poetic diction Aristotle[1] in his dry way had said more to the point in a few sentences twenty-one centuries before, when he observed that in poetry language too near daily life was liable to be clear but mean, while language too remote tended to be imposing but obscure; it therefore seemed wisest to aim at a happy mean. To which common-sense judgement he adds various qualifications for various kinds of poetry, no less sensible. And in the century before Coleridge, Johnson, at whom the Romantics were never tired of sneering, had put the essential point with his manly brevity: "Words being

[1] *Poetics*, XXII. Cf. also Horace, *Ars Poetica*, 45 ff.; Longinus, *passim*; Ben Jonson, *Timber*; Hobbes, *Answer to Davenant*; Addison, *Spectator*, No. 285. (The three last are quoted in the section on "Style and Diction" in R. P. Cowl's useful *Theory of Poetry in England*.)

arbitrary, must owe their power to association, and have the influence, and that only, which custom has given them"—"words too familiar, or too remote, defeat the purpose of a poet". But Johnson does not offer the gin of transcendental jargon; he does not intoxicate; it is all said and understood in a moment—as clear as water—and what good is that?

To pass from Johnson to Coleridge is, indeed, to see in little, I think, what critics gained and lost with the coming of Romanticism. They became far more sensitive, more enthusiastic, less hide-bound by rules—in practical criticism the advance is plain; but they tended also to become gushing, bardolatrous, muddle-headed, and mysterious, with a fondness for windy and cloudy theories that we are still plagued with to this day. Neo-classic criticism doubtless had too much "reality-principle"; but their Romantic successors stagger terribly at times from lack of it. To put down Coleridge and open Johnson is like emerging from some stuffy *salon*, full of smoke and the pseudo-intellectual conversation of talkers shouting at one another and listening only to themselves, into the keen night air of London. The sentences of the *Lives of the Poets* ring out clear and strong as its flagstones underfoot. One breathes again. Johnson is often dull-eared; often wrong-headed; but he seldom utters nonsense, and cant never. However, I believe in Bentley's "no man was ever written down except by himself", of which Bentley was himself to provide so terrible an example in his *Milton*: and I do not wish to seem to generalize, in my turn, without evidence. The following instances of Coleridge's judgement speak mostly for themselves.

"No man was ever yet a great poet without being a profound philosopher."[1] (How far can Sappho, Pindar, Catullus, Virgil, Chaucer, or even Milton, be called "*profound* philosophers"? And Shakespeare? Without going to the extreme of Mr Bernard Shaw and denying him "any ideas worth twopence", can we resist a suspicion of Romantic gush when he is called "the morning star, the guide and the pioneer, of true philosophy"?[2] What *was* Shakespeare's philosophy?)

"The clear and reciprocal connexion of just taste with pure morality."[3] (Without joining the extremists who deny all connection between art and life, one may hesitate to deny "taste" to a great many characters who would not have reached the distinctly prudish moral standards of Coleridge; who was shocked by the Widow Wadman and thought that Hazlitt, "poor wretch!", was "a melancholy instance of the awful Truth—that man cannot be on a level with the Beasts—he must be above them or below them".[4] Had Aristophanes, Catullus, Villon, Ronsard, Racine, Molière, Dryden, Diderot, Chateaubriand, Musset, Baudelaire, Sainte-Beuve, Rossetti no "just taste"? It was in the irony of things that Coleridge himself was destined to be condemned by Arnold as having "no morals"; surely a judgement in its turn far too hard on one who could at least inspire devoted friendship to the last.)

"In the strict sense of the word, an undevout poet is an impossibility."[5] Lucretius, we learn, is a mere verse-

---

[1] *Biog. Lit.* xv. [2] *Lit. Rem.* ii, 83. [3] *Lit. Rem.* ii, 62.
[4] *Unpub. Lett.* ii, 190. [5] Raysor, ii, 148.

maker; but the true poet is like "a child". It would be
an insult to the reader's intelligence to enumerate the
poets, from Euripides to Housman, who if not openly
"of the Devil's party" were certainly not of God's. "La
terre", writes Alfred de Vigny, "est révoltée des injustices
et de la création.... Tous ceux qui luttèrent contre le
ciel injuste ont eu l'admiration et l'amour secret des
hommes." Vigny was himself one of them; he exaggerated; but he exaggerated a truth. If Coleridge believed
what he said about the impossibility of an undevout
poet, how could he bring himself to write like this to
Byron (March 30th, 1815)?—"A sort of pre-established
good will, not unlike that with which the Swan instinctively takes up the weakly cygnet into the Hollow
between its wings, I knew I might confidently look for
from one who is indeed a Poet; were I but assured that
your Lordship had ever thought of me as a fellow-laborer
in the same vineyard, and as not otherwise unworthy
your notice. And surely a fellow-laborer I *have* been,
and a co-inheritor of the same Bequest, tho' of a smaller
portion." Imagine Johnson comparing himself to a
"weakly cygnet"! But with Coleridge it was too true;
and his swan-song was already sung.

"I wish our clever young poets would remember my
homely definitions of prose and poetry; that is, prose—
words in their best order;—poetry, the *best* words in the
best order."[1] ("Best" for what? For prose, or poetry,
presumably. Could good prose be "not the best words

---

[1] *Table Talk*, July 12th, 1827. Elsewhere (*T.T.*, July 3rd, 1833) "the
definition of good prose is—proper words in their proper places;—of
good verse—the most proper words in their proper places".

in not the best order"? What do we learn by this sort of circular statement?)

"In dramatic composition the observation of the unities of time and place so narrows the period of action, so impoverishes the sources of pleasure, that of all the Athenian dramas there is scarcely one in which the absurdity is not glaring, of aiming at an object and utterly failing in the attainment of it."[1]

(It is interesting to watch the Romantic becoming just as narrowly intolerant towards Classic rules as the neo-Classics towards Romantic licence. But, for some reason, Coleridge could not find "anything sublime" in Greek. Similarly, he talks lightheartedly of Greek actors' voices being "unnaturally and unmusically stretched" owing to the size of their theatres;[2] "hence the introduction of recitative, for the purpose of rendering pleasantly artificial the *distortion of the face*, and straining of the voice, occasioned by the magnitude of the building."[3] He had forgotten they wore masks!)

"The Greeks, except, perhaps, in Homer, seem to have had no way of making their women interesting, but by unsexing them, as in the instances of the tragic Medea, Electra, etc."[4] (He contrasts Spenser's Una. But if Spenser's Una is to be called "interesting", it seems a little hard to rule out Greek figures so living, although feminine, as Cassandra, Dejanira, Alcestis,

---

[1] Raysor, II, 161.

[2] Actually in a Greek theatre like that of Epidaurus the acoustics are so admirable that an ordinary speaking voice is audible everywhere. But Coleridge could be forgiven for not knowing that.

[3] Raysor, II, 73.   [4] *Lit. Rem.* I, 95.

Phaedra, Iphigenia, the witch-girl of Theocritus, or the young Medea of Apollonius, who helped to inspire Virgil's Dido.)

This coldness towards things Greek provides a strange contrast to the religious and Romantic fervour excited in Coleridge by anything Shakespearian; until again one sighs for the level-headedness of Johnson. "Shakespeare", we are told, "never introduces a word, or thought, in vain or out of place:[1] if we do not understand him, it is our fault or the fault of copyists and typographers." Not only is Shakespeare "the morning-star of true philosophy"; even his indecencies are somehow immaculate. "I appeal to the whole of Shakespeare's writings, whether his grossness is not the mere sport of fancy dissipating low feelings by exciting the intellect."[2] It is, of course, possible that some Elizabethans were wrong in not sharing Coleridge's view of *Venus and Adonis* as being totally unsensual, "like the twinkling dances of two vernal butterflies". But anyone who has studied Elizabethan drama comes to know how many *double-entendres* obscured by time are still skated over by delicate commentators; hardly one of whom dares to explain, for example, the last lines of the *Merchant of Venice*. There

---

[1] One's confidence in Coleridge's judgement on such a point is a little shaken by finding, in *Antony and Cleopatra,* how he proposes to emend

> Her gentlewomen, like the Nereides,
> So many mermaids....

As "mermaid" recurs two lines later, "I strongly suspect that Shakespeare wrote either 'sea-queens' or rather 'sea-brides'". Alternatively he suggests "submarine graces". (Raysor, I, 88.) It is on a par with his "evident" emendation of Doll Tear-sheet to "Tear-street" (*terere stratum*—"to walk the streets"!).

[2] Raysor, II, 127.

is no need to labour the point; but to gloss it over is cant. And since cant brings its own reward, we find Coleridge consequently driven to give notice of dismissal to that low Porter of Macbeth's. He must be a creature dragged in by the actors; apart from a single sentence, "not one syllable has the ever-present being of Shakespeare". Then, when that masterpiece of sardonic humour has thus been censored, we read that there is an "entire absence of comedy, nay, even of irony and philosophic contemplation, in *Macbeth*—because wholly tragic".[1]

Similarly with his view of Shakespeare's women. "'Most women have no character at all,' said Pope, and meant it for satire. Shakespeare, who knew man and woman much better, saw that it, in fact, was the perfection of woman to be characterless. Every one wishes a Desdemona or Ophelia for a wife—creatures who, though they may not always understand you, do always feel you, and feel with you."[2] When one is told that Coleridge "was naturally a psychologist", this passage among others recurs to memory. It may be replied that such cases are too practical. The excuse does not seem to me very good. If we are told that a man is a marvellous architect, but observe that his buildings repeatedly blow down, or have their staircases forgotten, we shrug our shoulders and go elsewhere. Psychologists, like architects, have plenty of scope for showing their "natural" gifts; the question is, how will their theories *work*?

Thus to like women "characterless" is a matter of taste; to say Shakespeare liked them so is rather bold;

[1] Raysor, I, 75, 78. And no "irony"?—with all the tragic irony of the Witches or of III, I, 36 ff. And why no irony *because* tragic?

[2] *Table Talk*, September 27th, 1830.

but to say that he actually drew them so and meant Ophelia to seem "perfect" or that "everyone" would like to marry her...! Even poor Desdemona, by a certain too delicate and fragile disingenuousness, does something to help on a tragedy that could hardly have occurred with Juliet or Rosalind or Portia; and as for Ophelia, it is strange indeed that Coleridge, who thought he had "a smack of Hamlet" himself, should have failed to see the essential part that poor charming doll surely plays in the final ruin at Elsinore. With his mother and uncle, Hamlet has lost faith in the loyalty of wife to husband, of brother to brother, of mother to son. He turns despairingly to the loyalty of friends—but Rosencrantz and Guildenstern are spies. To the loyalty of a mistress—but Ophelia (how different if it had been Juliet, or even Desdemona!) is ready to drop him at a parent's word; ready in her dreadful, docile innocence to spy likewise upon him. She too is part of this universal web of falsity; like her father, preaching "To thine own self be true" to the very son he is about to spy on in Paris; like her brother, preaching "honour" to her over whose very grave he is to rant, before he goes to do murder with his poisoned rapier. Ophelia too belongs to this world of lies, where for sixpence players howl as if their hearts would break for Hecuba; where young Osric is as ready as old Polonius to fawn assent, while the plot is being spun and the poison mixed. Ophelia is another Gertrude, lovely, innocent as yet, but spineless; that resemblance may even be the reason why it is from Gertrude that we hear the story of Ophelia's death. If Hamlet in his frenzy at the treachery all round him treats her as a prostitute, surely we are meant to feel that a girl less "characterless" would as little have provoked such treatment as endured it.

But Coleridge thought her perfect; just as he would needs have Falstaff valiant, not a coward (he "pretended to be one"); just as he is edified by Prince Hal's casting off of his old friend—here, "as in other instances, Shakespeare has showed us the defeat of mere intellect by a noble feeling, the Prince being the superior moral character who rises above his insidious companion".[1] Is this what most readers feel? Or, again, does one who is "naturally a psychologist" write to his own wife, one wonders, by way of soothing her jealousy of Dorothy Wordsworth and his friends?—"Permit me, my dear Sara, without offence to you, as Heaven knows! it is without any feeling of pride in myself, to say, that in six acquirements, and in quantity and quality of natural endowments whether of feeling, or of intellect, you are the inferior."[2] No wonder Coleridge thought Milton's docile Eve the only woman character comparable with Shakespeare's.

Next we are told that Shakespeare drew no misers because misers have become extinct, and he foresaw they would. "As a passion, avarice has disappeared. How admirably then did Shakespeare foresee that if he drew such a character, it could not be permanent!"[3] Apart from the question whether Shylock was not avaricious, is it in fact true that "avarice has disappeared"? And how could Shakespeare have foreseen it, anyway? And why, if so, did he choose to represent witches, who were surely nearer to extinction than misers?

[1] Raysor, II, 210.   [2] *Unpub. Lett.* I, 221.
[3] Raysor, II, 145.

Then we are asked to admire Shakespeare's artistic economy—"Schiller has the material sublime; to produce an effect he sets you a whole town on fire.... But Shakespeare drops a handkerchief."[1] This sounds so neat that most people assume instantly that it must be true. "A striking contrast," observes Saintsbury. But if one really considers all the battles and sieges and shipwrecks and hurricanes on blasted heaths, all the heaped-up corpses at the end of *Lear* and *Othello* and *Hamlet*, is it, in fact, the case? Why remember only Desdemona's handkerchief falling on the floor, and forget that "vile jelly", old Gloucester's eye? Is it not saner to admit that Shakespeare, like Nature, is magnificently extravagant; instead of praising him as if he were the author of *Bérénice*? Surely Shakespeare is more like the God of Peer Gynt—"God, I see, is still a father to me; but economical He is not."

For Coleridge, however, in the teeth of some fairly good evidence, Shakespeare must even have been a great actor. "It is my persuasion", he said to J. P. Collier, "—indeed my firm conviction—so firm that nothing can shake it—the rising of Shakespeare's spirit from the grave, modestly confessing his own deficiencies, could not alter my opinion—that Shakespeare, in the best sense of the word, was a very great actor. Great dramatists make great actors.... It is worth having died two hundred years ago to have heard Shakespeare deliver a single line."[2]

Great dramatists make great actors? Who, for example? What can one do with such methods of reasoning? Yet Saintsbury can say: "Coleridge never admires

[1] *T.T.*, December 29th, 1822.   [2] Raysor, II, 30 *n*.

Shakespeare too much." Such is Romantic criticism. You cannot trust it.

The same recklessness shows itself in details. Bolingbroke says:

> Go to the rude ribs of that ancient castle,
> Through brazen trumpet send the breath of parle
> Into his ruin'd ears. . . .

"Shakespeare", observes Coleridge, "purposely used the personal pronoun 'his', to show that although Bolingbroke was only speaking of the castle, his thoughts dwelt on the King."[1] "Ruin'd ears" may certainly apply as much to Richard as the castle; but everyone knows that in Shakespeare's day "its" was only just creeping into use; "his" is not necessarily a "personal pronoun" at all, being the regular possessive also of the *impersonal* pronoun "it". Elsewhere a similar false subtlety suggests to Coleridge that "Swift adopted the name Stella, which is a man's name, with a feminine termination, to denote the mysterious epicene relation in which poor Miss Johnston stood to him".[2] Stella is indeed a man's name in Latin; but how curious to forget the Stella of Sidney's Sonnets! Such slips do not matter in a poet; in a critic they may well give us pause. Yet it is far less these details that wake distrust than his habit of facile generalization on all subjects. Thus this "natural psychologist" tells us that "Humour is consistent with pathos, while wit is not".[3] Is there then no pathos in the dying wit of Mercutio; in Heine's "Dieu me pardonnera, c'est son métier"; in Oscar Wilde's "Robbie, I'm dying beyond my means"? Again, we

---

[1] Raysor, ii, 190.   [2] *T.T.*, July 26th, 1830.
[3] *Addit. T.T.* (Ashe), p. 326.

are impressively informed: "A true poem must give 'as much pleasure in each part as is compatible with the greatest sum of pleasure in the whole.'... In reading Milton, for instance, scarcely a line can be pointed out which, critically examined, could be called in itself good."[1] Open Milton anywhere: is it true? What shall we call "in itself good", if not lines like these?—

> Fall'n Cherube, to be weak is miserable....

> To bellow through the vast and boundless Deep....

> Thick as Autumnal Leaves that strew the Brooks
> In Vallombrosa....

> They heard, and were abasht, and up they sprung....

> The haunt of Seales and Orcs and sea-mews' clang....

> Eyeless in Gaza at the mill with slaves.

For a number of readers Milton lives by such isolated splendours rather than by his total effects; others will disagree; but who else will be found to praise his total effects and yet deny him great lines? Similarly, it is legitimate, though odd, for a critic to be blind to Wordsworth's daffodils. But it is difficult to respect a man who accuses the poem of "mental bombast" on the Pecksniffian ground that such words of ecstasy should be reserved to "describe the joy of retrospection, when the images and virtuous actions of a whole well-spent life pass before that conscience which is indeed the *inward* eye: which is indeed '*the bliss of solitude*'".[2] It is a curious picture of a happy afternoon's diversion. And when one reflects what Coleridge had done with his own talents,

[1] *Raysor*, II, 68.   [2] *Biog. Lit.* XXII.

while it would be heartless and priggish to reproach him overmuch, do we not wonder a little that he could without wincing write these complacent words?

I know that to criticize Coleridge's criticism will seem, to many, blasphemy; I remember how a coloured gentleman to whom I expressed doubts of his oracle's infallibility, turned paler and hastened away in horror before a thunderbolt should hurtle through the roof. But it seems to me a very small service to literature or to education to go on being so uncritical of this sort of criticism. Certainly Coleridge cannot claim to have been over-charitable to others. French criticisms of Shakespeare were for him "the judgments of monkeys by some wonderful phenomenon put into the mouths of people shaped like men".[1] (Indeed, the whole French nation was, he said, "like grains of gunpowder—each by itself smutty and contemptible".[2]) Hume, on the same subject of Shakespeare, resembled "an apothecary's phial placed under the falls of Niagara".[3] Voltaire was "a wretched sciolist"[4] and a "paltry scribbler". Of Buffon Coleridge "could not think without horror". Gay's *Beggar's Opera* filled him "with horror and disgust".[5] Johnson was "the Frog-Critic. How nimbly it leaps, how excellently it swims—only the fore-legs (it must be admitted) are too long, and the hind ones too short."[6] "Gibbon's style is detestable, but his style is not the worst thing about him."[7] Landor had never learned "how to write simple and lucid English".[8] Goethe was inferior to Schiller; and much of *Faust* "vulgar, licentious

---

[1] Raysor, II, 169.   [2] Raysor, II, 210.
[3] *T.T.*, July 30th, 1831.   [4] *Lit. Rem.*, II, 69.
[5] *Omniana* (1888), p. 387.   [6] Raysor, I, 82.
[7] *T.T.*, August 15th, 1833.   [8] *T.T.*, January 1st, 1834.

and blasphemous".[1] Scott's *Ivanhoe* and "*The Bride of
Ravensmuir*, or whatever its name may be" were "two
wretched abortions".[2] And Tennyson did not "very
well understand what metre was".[3] All critics, even
the greatest, have made their slips; but why are we never
allowed to forget Johnson's deafness to *Lycidas*, while
these observations of Coleridge's are delicately ignored?
Is it because the admirable later prose of Johnson can still
be revisited with pleasure, while his successor is largely
talked about by people who would rather praise than
read him?

Romanticism enabled Coleridge to write a poem more
poetic than anything for a hundred years before it; it
opened worlds to him that Johnson had never dreamed
of; but it also enabled him, in this new age with its
weakened sense of fact and of dignity, to write other
things also, that Johnson would never have dreamed of,
and some that Johnson would have scorned. "So then,"
writes Saintsbury, "there abide these three, Aristotle,
Longinus, and Coleridge."

It is forbidden to doubt this. The ordinary man is too
highbrow-beaten. And Coleridge suits admirably those
persons with religious instincts who want not critics but
mystagogues; who care not for the truth of what they
are told, but for its tune. They like what sounds profound,
even if it is largely lobbing pebbles down an empty well.
They would far rather read Coleridge than Sainte-
Beuve. But I suspect Coleridge of being a better
hypnotist than critic. "It is indeed a strange thing,"

[1] *T.T.*, February 16th, 1833.   [2] *Addit. T.T.*, January, 1821.
[3] *T.T.*, April 24th, 1833.

mused the Lady Murasaki in Japan a thousand years
ago, "that a perfectly ordinary remark, if made in a quiet
colourless voice, may seem original and interesting; for
instance, in conversations about poetry, some quite
commonplace piece of criticism will be accepted as
profound, merely because it is made in a particular tone
of voice".

The genius of Coleridge, it seems to me, remains
wonderful enough for what it was, without rhapsodies
over what it was not.

CHAPTER V

CRITICISM IN AN UNROMANTIC AGE

THREE years ago I was at Thermopylae. The mists clung low, I remember, on the slopes of Othrys and Oeta. Under the cold grey of the sky a chime of unseen goat-bells rose and sank, like a ghostly music, over pastures pale with asphodel; and a blue smoke of burning crawled heavily across the swamps of the Spercheios—the same Spercheios still to whom the old Peleus vowed the locks of Achilles, the day he should come safe home from Troy. Eastward lay the misty strait of Artemision, up which the Persian came; and, hidden behind Euboea, that rocky Scyros where rested, once, the dust of Theseus and now of Rupert Brooke. In Greece the dead past walks so living in the light of noon, that the present itself seems often more ghostly by its side. And there at the Gate of Thermopylae the thought of those quiet lines of Simonides on the most famous of all forlorn hopes for freedom—

> Tell them at Lacedaemon, passer-by,
> That here obedient to their laws we lie—

calls up, as something very faint and far away, the thought of modern Europe, fast growing too Spartan to be free; beside the memory of Homer's Achilles in his eternal youth there rises like a pale and fretful ghost the memory of that modern poetry which proclaims itself a whimper of hollow men, and of the modern critics who applaud it as the true utterance of a disillusioned age.

What is it that has happened to our poetry, and our judges of poetry, in the twenty years since Rupert Brooke, silent now in Scyros, was writing verse which, whatever its lasting worth, at least quivered with vitality; and prose, above all in his letters, that danced with such grace and gaiety on the threshold of the world? It is easy to reply—"The War". More has happened than that—so much, that qualities like his are hardly even considered now in the philosophy of critics. So impossible does it seem for any two successive generations to agree what they mean by the simple statement—"This poem is good." What indeed does it mean?

To the Greek in his best days good poetry meant, above all, poetry that bred good men. The Muses were the daughters of Omniscience. The God of Poetry was the God also of Prophecy and of Healing, the divine voice that spoke at the Delphic centre of the earth. How to plough, how to fight, how to live, how to die—the poets taught all these. The boy who got by heart the great speech of Sarpedon, the girl who heard recited the farewell of Hector to Andromache, might learn, so the Greek believed, how themselves to face hereafter the breaking-points of life. And, even when the day of Greece draws to its twilight, reading Plutarch we might feel that this belief had not been belied by the lives their greatest led; reading "Longinus" we shall find the same faith unrepentantly repeated in that treatise *On Great Writing* which rings like a funeral oration over the literature of his race—"Great writing is the echo of a great soul." Now, of course, so naïve a view is quite exploded; no one supposes that art can have to do with ethics, or poetry be anything so absurd as a sort of morals set to music.

The men of the Middle Ages, however, still believed something of the kind, though they spun few theories about it. For, even more than antiquity, the Middle Ages did almost wholly without critics; and, by some miracle, did quite well without. But in Dante's eyes, for example, the three great subjects for poetry must still be the three fundamental things—Salus, Venus, Virtus— War by which life is defended, Love by which it is perpetuated, Conduct by which it is controlled. The Morality Plays, again, only too conscientiously earn their name. For "moral Gower", as for Horace, a poem is "good" that mixes profit with pleasure—

> wisdom to the wise
> And pley to hem that lust to pleye.

And for Malory, as for his publisher Caxton, the tale of Arthur has a purpose to serve, a high and reproachful example to set before a chivalry grown decadent.

But there is one important change. In Greece, when a clash occurs, it is the moralist who rebels against the poet—Xenophanes against Homer, Solon against Thespis, Plato against all poetry; in the Middle Ages, when Christianity dominates Europe and the Church has built in the Catholic West something not wholly unlike the city of Plato's dream, it is the poet, now half an outlaw, who turns at times to kick against the pricks of a tyrannical morality. When the Wandering Scholars steal for the tavern the rhythms of the choir, when Aucassin gaily prefers Hell with its harpers and minstrels to the bleak Heaven of priest and anchorite, when from brothel or gibbet rings out the wild voice of Villon, a new race stands on the frontiers of literature—the Bohemians.

With the Renaissance arrive also, in full force, the Critics. Their endeavour is double—to save literature from the ethical attacks of Plato and the Puritans; and to subject it instead to the aesthetic rules of Aristotle and the Pedants. To be "good", Poetry must now observe the Laws of God on the one hand and of the Ancients on the other; but especially of the Ancients.

Then against these Ancients, as the Renaissance in its turn grows old, the Moderns grow rebellious. The classical scholar begins to carry less weight than the man of the world, a Bentley than a Dryden or an Addison. By an easy compromise it becomes the orthodox creed to believe in a new Trinity of three things which yet are one—the wisdom of the Ancients, Nature, and Good Sense—the three benign powers that had fashioned this ordered world of neo-Classicism out of the benighted chaos of Monk and Goth. Never had it been so easy to know what was good poetry, and what was not; never was it to be so easy again. Critics were judges administering the law of an enlightened land. They still disagreed, being human; but about the applications, not the principles, of the law. Racine voices his delight at finding by actual experience that Good Sense was indeed the same in ancient Athens as in modern Paris. Nearly a century later Thomas Warton can still speak, without irony, of living "in the days of writing by rule", when "critical taste is universally diffused". We amid our critical anarchy may mingle with our amusement a touch, perhaps, of regret.

Unfortunately, if it had become easy to say what was good poetry, it had become strangely rare to write it. Upon this world so comfortably reposing on its false premisses came the retribution of revolution. Excess became wisdom; exuberance, beauty. After that Romantic riot had passed, the nineteenth century restored a certain reign of order in literature; but never the reign of law that the eighteenth had known. Matthew Arnold, for example, was respected, not obeyed. He might condemn modern writers as "fantastic" and "lacking in sanity"; he might demand that poetry should be "criticism of life". In answer came the shout of "Art for Art's sake", and a new invasion of Bohemians or of aesthetes seeking not so much the defiant Hell of Aucassin as an Epicurean Olympus of their own. To-day that war-cry too has died away; and we hear only, like Virgil's doomed warrior out in No Man's Land:

Confusae sonus urbis et inlaetabile murmur—
The voice of a city's trouble, and a murmur void of joy.

For Antiquity, in a word, "good" poetry meant noble poetry. For the Renaissance it meant learned poetry; the poetry of scholars, and of wits. For the eighteenth century it became the poetry of men—and women—of the world. For the Romantics, the poetry of generous rebels. They still had rules, if only to break them. But now—! Twenty-three centuries after the Father of Criticism, Aristotle, is there a single law of literature, a single principle for writing poetry, a single canon for criticizing it, about which a congress of our critics would agree? For it is no longer agreed that poetry should be beautiful, or noble, or civilized, or well constructed, or musical, or intelligent, or even intelligible. If criticism be a science, only contrast its progress with that of any other. We know nothing. Unhappily, unlike Socrates, we do not seem to know even that. It would indeed be much to expect. The multiplication of sects is not apt to multiply tolerance. It is only natural that criticism, growing more chaotic, should grow more dogmatic too. To-day we hear with admiration that *Hamlet* is "most certainly"—"most certainly an artistic failure"; or again, in painting, that El Greco can be *proved* a greater painter than Velasquez. It might seem sometimes as if critics were doomed to remain the Bourbons of the world of Art—forgetting nothing, learning nothing. And while they persist in talking as if the values they now discover in poetry were the obvious and only ones, the values themselves grow odder and odder. Thus a panegyric by a modern critic on Mr Ezra Pound, after celebrating the poet's subtlety in the use of inverted commas, proceeds: "His poise, though so varied, and for all his audacities, is sure; how sure, nothing can show better than the pun in the last stanza of the third poem:

> O bright Apollo,
> τίν' ἄνδρα, τίν' ἥρωα, τίνα θεόν,[1]
> What god, man, or hero
> Shall I place a tin wreath upon!"

[1] The above is printed as in the original, with the usual dose of solecisms—not the least characteristic side of Mr Pound's passion for Greek. The curious reader should turn to the *Selected Poems* of Mr Ezra Pound, edited by Mr T. S. Eliot. Here he will find two master-minds of our age in conjunction; and, finding also one classical howler after another, may admire the intuition which enables Mr Pound, in a manual of universal culture entitled *How to Read*, to dismiss Thucydides as "a journalist", and to "chuck out" Pindar "without the slightest compunction".

(Since the above was written, I have received from Mr Pound, who is a total stranger to me, a letter, ungrammatical in its English and unprintable in its vocabulary, informing me that I was "born in infamy" and breathing threats of violence, because I had written to the press on behalf of the unfortunate Abyssinians. *Tout se tient*.)

"In what poet, after the seventeenth century," continues the critic, "can we find anything like this contributing to a completely serious effect (the poem is not only tragically serious but solemn)!" "τίν᾽ ἄνδρα"—"tin wreath"—the sort of joke made by preparatory school-boys beginning Greek—"sureness of poise"—"not only tragically serious but solemn"! Solemn?—Yes. A belfry full of owls could not equal it. But, as wit, surely Slender himself would have found it a little thin?

Little wonder, in this welter of opinions, if a critic as honest as Dr I. A. Richards has given up his earlier attempt to devise a criterion of values; abjured in his *Practical Criticism* all principles for judging poetry, "however refined and subtle"; and declared that it is the reader's business to value works for himself, while the critic's sole concern is with interpretation.

That interpretation remains by far his most important function may well be; but is it all? Instead of saying "I think this poem is good" should he really say, like that precise gentleman, the Abbé de Saint-Pierre, "Cela est bon, pour moi, quant à présent"?

For a long time, indeed, I thought so—that calling a poem "good" did in fact mean simply "I value it"; or "many educated people have valued it for many years past"; or, if it was a new work, "I think many educated people will value it for many years to come." A critical judgement was, in other words, either autobiography, or history, or a guess about the future. Thus when Matthew Arnold called Shelley "an ineffectual angel", it was a defiance of history and a bad prophecy—Shelley has had far too much effect to be called that; but it remained a very interesting piece of critical autobiography, by no means deserving the angry abuse that has been hurled at it. For to a whole class of men from Lamb onwards—men quite as sensitive to poetry as others—Shelley *has* seemed, in Mr Max Beerbohm's phrase, "a crystal crank". Any sort of absolute Beauty, in other words, like absolute Good, I have always failed to believe in. The impression a poem gives seems to me like a child begotten by the poet's thought on the reader's, in "a marriage of true minds". Two readers can no more have identical impressions than two mothers could have identical children. Indeed, to adapt Heraclitus, even the same person cannot read the same poem twice—he will have changed in the interval. A hundred biologists will see essentially the same caterpillar, because men have essentially the same eyes, and the same way of reasoning to check their data. But we do not look at poetry through microscopes. It builds itself a body next our hearts, out of memories and emotions that are ours alone. That is why it is so hard to make the Art of Criticism in any sense a science.

And yet are there no standards? Is there no relation to be found between these apparent caprices within us and the laws that seem to govern the world outside?—no series of intricate cog-wheels by which our instinctive preferences may fit ultimately into the mesh of the great wheel of things? For if the differences between human beings are extraordinary, so also are the fundamental likenesses, the experiences that we can and do somehow share; so that after three thousand years Homer and Sappho still fascinate remote barbarians like ourselves, who do not even know how to pronounce the music of their verse. When values have stood so firm, can we find no foundations beneath them? And when, on the other hand, we are summoned to go down on our knees before hollow men or tin wreaths, can we only agree to differ? Or when a critic, contrasting Baudelaire with Tennyson, singles out for special praise that worst poem of Baudelaire's which describes the swarming of flies and maggots on a woman's putrid corpse, and explains that *In Memoriam* fails because Tennyson himself failed to picture Arthur Hallam lying like that in Clevedon churchyard, can one only say to this sort of imbecile—"Well, if you like that kind of thing, I suppose it's good for you"? Because one knows it isn't.

Some criterion, in fact, some standard of judgement can, I think, be found. Often it cannot be applied. It could very often be misapplied. But even an islet, even a single plank, is something to cling to in such a chaos.

The fundamental instinct of all life, we may say, is to extend and multiply itself—to live more abundantly, to live more complexly. Roots, polyps, philosophers, all stretch their feelers out and out into the unknown, straining to turn Not-Me into Me. And as the living organism acquires more memory and more consciousness, it is as if it planted flowers along the paths it had found best to follow—the flowers of pleasure; and along the paths to destruction, the thorns of pain. Then the creature may grow too absorbed in gathering roses, or primroses, to look where it is going—even though, in an ever-changing world, the primrose path leads now to a precipice. What was a signal of safety or of danger warns no longer: the means has become itself an end. Now we eat to please our palates; we love for loving's sake; we think for mere curiosity. The *savant* and the artist are born; eager to think and know and feel, to see and hear, for no satisfaction beyond the experience and the activity in themselves.

But to all this a Greek, I think, might have answered: "True, there are no fairer flowers than grow on the paths of the Muses. Yet Time will let no one stand still, and all paths lead somewhere. Therefore in Greece we always thought it simple sense to ask where such paths led. These flowers bear fruit; among them we have found growing the lotus and the hemlock. The art of men is like the play of animals; but the play of animals is not only play; it is a rehearsal of life, a quickening of eye and a strengthening of sinew for struggles to come. When a human play is over and the actors doff their masks, life still remains to be lived. Your cleverest critics will say that a work is 'improbable' or 'tedious' or 'badly written'; that it is 'well-constructed' or 'brilliant' or 'intoxicating'. There they stop. But our Aristophanes did not question that Euripides was brilliant; he was concerned because he thought him a brilliant will-o'-the-wisp—and the more brilliant, the worse. He did not deny he was intoxicating; he denied that intoxication was of necessity a good state of mind. He was wrong, you say? But wrong in principle? He was one-sided? Are you so sure you are not?

"Do your critics really show much breadth of vision, when they talk so much of the tricks of the trade—of the heating of the pastry-cook's oven and the mixing of the dough; and never stop to ask if his products are wholesome or poison in the end? We hear a great deal of the fiddler's cat-gut and the skill of his fingering; not whether his music is the sort that Helots or harlots love.

"You are tolerant—or indifferent—about these things. But you, or your posterity, may find that Nature is not."

Now I confess it does not seem to me altogether easy to answer this Greek. And yet does this mean that we have run full circle round the corner into the hands of Plato, once more, and into the arms of Mrs Grundy? Are we handing over Poetry to be strait-laced by the Puritans on the one hand, prostituted for propaganda on the other by Fascist and Communist? That would be appalling. Yet Greek poetry escaped. Why?

There are, I think, certain human qualities that we have learnt spontaneously to value, because life has proved them valuable. This instinctive admiration is like the instinctive pleasure we take in other wholesome things; but more disinterested, more aesthetic. Vitality, strength, courage, devotion, pity, grace—these move us, as directly as beauty moves us. But not, surely, without cause. When a woman loves a man's strength or courage, it is only because her dead ancestors, sitting in council within her, push her blindly with their ghostly hands towards what she will need, for herself and her children, in the warfare of the world. So with the instinctive appeal such qualities possess in general—it is no mere whimsy or matter of taste. We think courage a fine and poetic thing, for the excellent, if prosaic, reason that it has been for ages untold a highly important thing to have.

In other words it is hard to say where exactly aesthetics ends and ethics begins. The Greeks felt that truth so intuitively that they used one word, which we poorly render "fine", to express both the "good" and the "beautiful". For the same reason their poetry and their morality closely overlapped. The root of good living, for them, was to temper good sense with poetic imagination; the root of good poetry, to temper poetic imagination with good sense. The same attitude stands out in what seems to me perhaps the noblest sculpture that I know—the West Pediment at Olympia. It is a scene of wild riot and rapine, the attempt of the Centaurs at the bridal of Peirithous to carry off the women of the Lapithae. One can imagine the turpitude and crudity for which such a subject would seem a heaven-sent occasion now. But there at Olympia even the bestial Centaurs have acquired instead a touch of that nobility of suffering, which Shakespeare in his gracious wisdom gave even to Caliban. And amidst all the heat and dust of that mad grapple of writhing bodies and clutching hands, of straining feet and gnashing teeth, the heroes and their women still keep upon their faces the unearthly calm of walkers in a dream. One woman, above all, is thrusting from her with magnificent force a Centaur's encircling arms; but her countenance, bent earthwards, not on him, is so still that it might have come from some statue of Meditation or of Solitude. In the centre of all, with one arm stretched above the tumult, stands the very embodiment of the Greek spirit, Apollo, with the splendour of his immortal body, the calm, a little heavy even, of the gods that know no mortal pain. It is appalling that the Greek genius should ever have sunk from this to the grimacings of the Laocoon. But here at its highest at Olympia it recalls the saying of the French critic

Alain: "Les beaux visages sont comme des preuves de cette puissance d'oublier et de s'oublier. Je doute qu'on puisse citer un beau visage où l'on ne lise cette absence de préjugé, ce pardon à toutes choses et à soi, cette jeunesse enfin toujours jeune, qui vient de ce qu'on ne joue aucun personnage." That is too narrow a definition of beauty. But it is interesting that it might almost be a psycho-analyst's definition of mental health—a state of mind tormented by no repressions, no worms of conscience, no senses of guilt. So with Homer. Greek Art at its best seems to me, above all, and beyond all others, sane. And sanity, I think, is not a matter of taste.

But the end came—Plato, Christianity, asceticism, Puritanism. The great flaw in the Greek view of poetry had been that it was often too crudely didactic. They were over-simple. Like Ruskin after them, they failed sometimes to see that Poetry had far better imply things than preach them directly—that in the open pulpit her voice grows hoarse and fails. And now new moralities arose that considered not health, but holiness; not sanity, but sin. As morality lost its poetry, poetry tended to lose its morale; to the ultimate undoing of both. The revolt of Aucassin may indeed be stimulating at first; but I doubt if either Bohemia or Ivory Towers are healthy for poets in the end. Ivory Towers have Ivory Gates, through which false and vain dreams come. Such a life divides the poet from his hearers; it divides him against himself. Even Milton's Paradise was all the more lost because its creator was himself half of the Devil's party. Milton's indeed is a typical dilemma, like Spenser's, like Matthew Arnold's, torn between the splendour of the Hellene and the Hebrew's righteousness. It is good, they feel, to turn the other cheek; yet it is fine "never to submit or yield".

> Martha I paint, and dream of Hera's brow;
> Mary, and think of Aphrodite's form.

But in spite of this recurrent clash for two thousand years between ethic and aesthetic ideals, certain qualities that we value in real life still affect, more than we often realize ourselves, the value we attach even to so technical a thing as style. Mr Yeats, who writes of poetry like a poet, not like a pedant or a priest, has spoken on this very point, of "that purification from insincerity, vanity, malignity, arrogance which is the discovery of style... style which is but high breeding in words and in argument". These qualities do not figure largely in the pages of critical treatises; which is perhaps partly why they never yet taught anyone to write. But in the style of the Epic Masters, for instance, from the *Iliad* to *The Dynasts*, amid all their differences, there seems to me always something nobly proud and aloof; upon their pages stands imprinted the shadowy footmark of the lion. Or take a more concrete example, a familiar pair of parallel passages, the dying speech of Arcite in Chaucer and in Dryden.[1]

> Naught may the woful spirit in myn herte
> Declare o poynt of alle my sorwes smerte
> To yow, my lady, that I love most;
> But I biquethe the service of my gost

[1] This was written before the delivery by Professor Housman of his Leslie Stephen Lecture for 1933, in which there occurs a similar comparison of other passages in the *Knight's Tale*, by Chaucer and by Dryden, with a similar conclusion. There indeed the comparison is made from the point of view of style alone. But it is pleasant to find this measure of confirmation from such an authority.

To yow aboven every creature,
Sin that my lyf may no lenger dure.
Allas, the wo! allas, the peynes stronge,
That I for yow have suffred, and so longe!
Allas, the deeth! alas, myn Emelye!
Allas, departyng of our companye!
Allas, myn hertes quene! allas, my wyf!
Myn hertes lady, endere of my lyf!
What is this world? what asketh men to have?
Now with his love, now in his colde grave
Allone, withouten eny companye.
Farwel, my swete fo! myn Emelye!
And softe tak me in your armes tweye,
For love of God, and herkneth what I seye.

Those eighteen lines Dryden improved to twenty-eight:

No language can express the smallest part
Of what I feel, and suffer in my heart,
For you, whom best I love and value most.

Chaucer's "woful spirit" has become, in Dryden,
"language". That change is but too symbolical of the
rest! Just as Dryden supposes, writing with the cleverness
of the head and not the wisdom of the heart, that "love
and value" means more than Chaucer's simple "love".

But to your service I bequeath my ghost;
Which, from this mortal body when untied,
Unseen, unheard, shall hover at your side;
Nor fright you waking, nor your sleep offend,
But wait officious, and your steps attend.

Dryden has dressed up into a sort of spectral footman
that forlorn hope of the dying Arcite which Chaucer had
wisely left in a sad brevity, vague as the hope itself.

How I have loved, excuse my faltering tongue,
My spirit's feeble, and my pains are strong;
This I may say, I *only* grieve to die,
Because I lose my charming Emily.

This Chaucer's Arcite did not say; with advantage, since when said we do not believe it.

> To die, when Heaven had put you in my power!
> Fate could not choose a more malicious hour.

Chaucer's Arcite did not talk about Heaven putting Emily "in his power", as if she were some captured animal; nor was he small enough to imagine Fate itself so small as to gratify "malice".

> What greater curse could envious Fortune give,
> Than just to die when I began to live!
> Vain men! how vanishing a bliss we crave;
> Now warm in love, now withering in the grave!

Here Dryden seems to me to be growing for a moment more sincere; then he again remembers his audience and his fatal itch to produce effects; and the falsetto returns.

> Never, O never more to see the sun!
> Still dark, in a *damp* vault, and still alone!

One would think he was afraid of catching, like Webster's Flamineo, "an everlasting cold".

> This fate is common; but I lose my breath
> Near bliss, and yet not blessed before my death.
> Farewell! but take me dying in your arms;
> 'Tis all I can enjoy of all your charms.

The anguish of a dying lover at leaving his mistress unpossessed is a touch true enough to life, though Chaucer passed it by; in the last letters of Keats it becomes terrible; but, tricked out with these flowers of speech, does it not become a little rancid, a little crude and vulgar? And, with ten lines more than Chaucer, how much of Chaucer's poetry Dryden has lost! If one cares for labels like Fancy and Imagination, I know no better example of the difference between them.

Dryden was surely an admirable journalist in verse; sometimes a splendid orator; occasionally a great poet. He had gained, from the poets before him and from his own fluent career, a greater familiarity than Chaucer could ever have, with the capacities of the heroic couplet and the English tongue. He was gifted with all the wit of the Metaphysical Poets, and with sense enough to abandon their abuse of it. Yet despite all these technical advantages comparison with Chaucer, as with Milton, kills him. It is like the contact of Satan with Ithuriel's spear—

for no falsehood can endure
Touch of celestial temper.

Dryden could be sincere; but often he did not choose to be. There was about his character this touch of the second-rate which reveals itself as inescapably in the lines of a poem as in the lines of a face. It is natural enough in an age when criticism of poetry cares for none of these things, thinking only of technique and of cleverness, that Dryden should be idolized and his reputation rise till *All for Love* is ranked with or above *Antony and Cleopatra*. With a similar extravagance we praise Donne; for, as Dryden salted life with clever wit, Donne spattered life with clever mud. That vein of cheapness, in spite of which these poets were justly honoured in the past, tends now to become their special merit in the eyes of critics who care not for the Donne who can be as direct as Catullus, as imaginatively lovely as Marvell, but for Donne the human corkscrew. In the same way Pope is promoted from his old place as a flashing wit, with a touch of the tragic intensity of the asp, to rank with those who seem to me companions for

a lifetime, where he is a companion for half-hours. The
man who wrote—

> Yes, I am proud, I must be proud to see
> Men not afraid of God, afraid of me—

does indeed attain for a moment the daemonic greatness
of Shakespeare's Iago; but that is rather different from
being Shakespeare. And when I hear thin-lipped persons praising Swift to the heavens, I am tempted to
wish them there, with their idol for company through
eternity. Swift with his tragic intensity may recall now
Lear, now Thersites. But does one not feel sometimes
that if life looks like that, it would be more intelligent
to hop over a cliff and be silent, than to go nagging
on for ever? Is there not something a little petty about
such peevishness? Chaucer can smile, even when the
heart of Troilus cracks; Shakespeare can jest, even when
Cleopatra comes to die. Swift had genius; but surely
genius is better when it is not also a disease?

Enough of examples. When one is pleading a case, the
great thing is not to claim too much. All I suggest is this.
We have reached a state of chaos in which all critical
standards of value have broken down. In the past there
have been too many; now there are none. Yet there
remain certain qualities that for three thousand years
men have valued alike in life and in what they have
agreed to call great literature—qualities which it has
become second nature to most normal minds to find
appealing, but which reason and experience also tell
us we do well to like. Nobility, intensity, courage,
generosity, pity—qualities like these cannot by them-

selves make a poem good, any more than they can make a face beautiful. Socrates looked like a Satyr; though I am sure it was a very charming Satyr. But in a poem, as in a face, no perfection of form in their absence can reach the highest beauty. And in a poem, as in a face, the presence of their opposites—of vulgarity or morbidity or poltroonery or meanness or cruelty—is a flaw for which no perfection of form can atone.

To a Greek this would have been, I think, obvious. Now it is no longer that. So much the worse for us. Unfortunately the moralists long ago began by picking a quarrel with poetry. The trouble with most moralists from Plato onwards is, I think, that they have been themselves so immoral. Neurotic themselves, they have bred neurotics to match them among the poets. For the values common to good living and good poetry seem to me not so much matters of what used to be called "virtue" as, above all, of sane vitality.

Not that one and the same scale of values will hold unchanged for the realm of the poetic imagination and for the real world. No doubt Milton or Michelangelo would have been ill to live with; Marlowe was no model citizen. Their energy was too vigorous for suburbs. But values vary even with earthly frontiers to some extent, between Paris and London; that is not to say they can therefore be ignored or turned topsy-turvy.

Nor need writers like Swift or Baudelaire be denied greatness, because there was so much about them neither sane nor sound. On the one hand, they still keep an intensity of passion however poisoned, an intensity of life however drunk with death, very different from the *lâcheté* and vulgarity, the whimperings and the clatter of tin wreaths, to which we have been treated since the War; on the other, they created nightmare worlds which our curiosity may well wish to visit, though not to inhabit; just as Odysseus devised how to hear the Sirens' song and would doubtless have managed to find his way into the Venusberg, had it existed then. But he would have managed there too—and here it is important to imitate him—not to fall under the fascination that can turn men to swine, not to forget his rugged Ithaca, "brave nursing-mother of men".

Nor is there any question of inventing some formula by which to approach the judgement of poetry. One does not feel by formula. But this does provide some means of checking and controlling our feelings about a poem by our feelings about life at large; just as in the realm of physical taste we control our instinctive liking for certain kinds of food, if we have any sense, by our other instinctive liking for good health. For our instincts can be fallible alone, and one must sometimes check another. I find it something, if only a pleasant illusion, to feel that judgements of the value of literature can bear *some* relation to the real world; and that one is not completely limited to saying, in effect—"In this sublime form of skittles called Poetry, you like blue skittles and I like red—and there's an end of it." These are, after all, not matters of such indifference. When we waver undecided between one sort of poetry and another, our eyes may be opened for a moment like those of Aeneas, when his mother showed him the mysterious shapes of the Immortals behind the reek of burning Troy; we may seem to see Nature casting into one scale Life itself and into the other Death, as Brennus cast his sword into the balance on the Capitol, with the cry, like him—"Vae victis!" For the qualities by which men have survived are hardly irrelevant to the survival of literature. One may doubt if it is to "hollow men" that the future world belongs.

Perhaps I may add that this theory did not begin as a theory, but because I have found by spontaneous experience more and more that even the aesthetic pleasure of a poem depends for me on the fineness of the personality glimpsed between its lines; on the spirit of which the body of a book is inevitably the echo and the mould. Herrick, for instance, is not heroic; he is, on the contrary, a superb example of the pure artist; and yet how his work would drop to dust without the graceful gaiety, the humour, and the humanity of the man himself behind! It is not what writers preach that matters; it is what they themselves are. More and more decidedly, as against work that is tainted with mania or cruelty or barbarism, one comes back to the vital and the sane, to Greek poetry, to Chaucer or the Ballads, to Ronsard or Shakespeare, to Keats or Morris or Hardy. And in moments of doubt about the value of a book, I find myself referring it in imagination to a ghostly jury, not of professional critics, but of men and women of this world. To it are invited Horace and Montaigne; the woman's wit of Dorothy Osborne, the sensitive simplicity of Dorothy Wordsworth; the eighteenth-century common sense of Horace Walpole and Madame Geoffrin; Landor with his stormy honesty and Hardy with his quiet irony. Of course, like Owen Glendower, one may call spirits from the vasty deep, and they may not come. Or I may badly mishear what they say. Certainly they often disagree. But would not any poet prefer such a tribunal, could it but be found, to twelve legions of professors? Do we honestly think Shakespeare would have quitted his "Mermaid" for our lecture-rooms?

And at least, if one is wrong in this refusal to put asunder the values of life and poetry, one is wrong in good company—with Milton who held that the poet's life should be a true poem; with Montaigne for whom the life of "toute âme bien née" seemed essentially that; with Anatole France who, sceptic though he was and devoid of literary principles, yet suggested that there was one quality common to the great masters—not style, nor composition, nor taste, but simply that "ils n'ont pas l'âme basse". And was not this, ultimately, what Matthew Arnold intended by poetry being "the criticism of life"? Yet what a dismal definition!—that poetry should be criticism of anything! Is it not rather life itself that is the final criticism of poetry?

What, then, of the critics?—what can they do, in practice, most worth doing? Granted that the critic's main business is interpretation, he may treat that as a science or as an art. To scientific critics, from Aristotle to the present day, the objection remains that poetry is a thing which works inside us, and we still know so extremely little about our insides. We may be now beginning to know more. But psychology is young and green as yet. Hitherto, even the generalizations of an Aristotle have worn threadbare in the end. And when some modern anatomist of poetry begins explaining— "This poem makes us feel like this, because..."—I find myself shouting vainly to his deaf page—"But, to begin with, it doesn't make me feel like that in the least." And when he proceeds, unperturbed—"So you see, what people have fondly called poetic magic, was this pretty little bag of tricks"—I cannot muster the profuse gratitude that seems expected in return for this revelation, even were it true. No doubt it is vain to follow Keats in drinking confusion to Newton; Einstein confuses *us*. Let us face the day when every leap of the heart that literature gives us shall be duly charted and analysed in coloured inks; but that day is not yet in sight. And I shall not pray for it. Its dawn may well prove a triumph for science rather than for art. The more we discover of what we call the "unconscious", the more we may doubt the benefit of dragging up into the light of consciousness impulses that for the poets and readers of three thousand years have worked unconsciously. They were wiser than they knew; we may not prove so much wiser when we know.

> They that in play can do the thing they would,
> Having an instinct throned in reason's place—
> And every perfect action hath the grace
> Of indolence or thoughtless hardihood—
> These are the best.[1]

Further, those who concentrate on these problems seem quickly to forget the existence in poetry of anything but technique. The eye grows short-sighted over the microscope; the voice of life calls deadened through a laboratory door. Scott (characteristically enough) in that great book, his *Journal*, tells of Michelangelo calling some Pope a poor creature, because his Holiness turned from

[1] Bridges.

the general effect of a noble figure to criticize the hem of its robe. So much the worse, I suppose, for Michelangelo. Yet one may ask if his form of exaggeration is not at least healthier than its opposite. In the Aran Islands, I gather, they believe that to talk too much of the things of fairy may turn the tongue to stone. It happens. I have seen it.

The critics who have mattered to me were themselves artists who turned literary criticism into literature. They brought to the study of poetry the imagination of poet and novelist in one. *Rasselas* and *The Vanity of Human Wishes* are not masterpieces of the first order; but they helped to make Johnson the most vital of English critics. *Volupté*, despite its title, is the dreariest novel I ever groaned through; in his poems Sainte-Beuve was little better; yet his criticism was all the better for both. These men had studied mankind too closely to fall into formulas, or to forget life in aestheticism. "The only end of writing", says Johnson, "is to enable the readers better to enjoy life, or better to endure it." "What I have sought in criticism", writes Sainte-Beuve, "has been to bring into it a certain charm, and at the same time more reality; in a word, both poetry and physiology." This sense of reality in poetry and of poetry in reality, is not an idle nor an easy quality. Taine may serve to show the effect of too much physiology; Coleridge, of too little reality.

Critical interpretation remains then, I feel, an art—an applied art like portrait-painting, or like translation—best handled by minds at once poetic and practical, like Horace and Montaigne, Dryden and Johnson, Goethe and Arnold; or, in our own day, Yeats and Virginia

Woolf, Lytton Strachey and Desmond MacCarthy. It was, above all, the poetry in the treatment of Greek and Latin literature by Gilbert Murray and Mackail, that planted with green for me at school the road to the originals. That this type of imaginative criticism has been badly abused, I know; that is no reason for abusing it. I know that the head of Pater's La Gioconda is ready to be brought in on a charger and pitched at me; but if we want a kind of criticism that shall be fool-proof, we must look to another world than this. And if this world is to continue habitable for civilized people, surely we need more, not less, mixing of poetry with the common ways of life.

That is where modern criticism of poetry, I think, has failed us. It is vain to expect too much of any criticism; as Arnold did. Men of the pen overrate the power of the pen. And where criticism has tried to lead the poets, as at the Renaissance, it has often only misled them. But if it be true that artists need a sense of values in life, critics —as artists judging artists—need it doubly. Yet the modern reviewer is usually afraid to say—"This poetry is clever, but its spirit is that of a rabbit imprisoned in a dust-bin"[1]—"This satire shows force, but it shows also a vulgar brutality with no sense of the dignity of others or its own". Critics now suppose such things irrelevant; or are afraid of being thought prigs or snobs. Yet the critic who does not feel the sheer aesthetic ugliness of such qualities is as incompetent as a colour-blind person in a picture-gallery. Poetry is not a jewel

[1] I have since been solemnly informed that though some modern poetry may adopt this tone, the poet is only pretending. In spite of this revelation, I still hold that a besetting taste for such impersonations reveals a good deal of the personality behind.

found in the heads of toads. And now in America, I hear, a school of critics has arisen to declare tragedy "out of date", because it needs heroic characters, and modern man has lost faith in his own value. As if Ibsen had not wrung more tragedy out of a wild duck in an attic than out of the fall of the whole ancient world in the face of Christianity! But to-day the individual cowers before Communist and Fascist, before scientist and engineer. Our age is disillusioned, so its intellectual leaders proudly and interminably tell us. What little worms we all are; and what clever little worms to know it so well! One modern poet, in verses peculiarly admired, has lamented that he was not born a healthy lobster. And this sort of neurotic cant is called "sincerity"—the one moral quality ceaselessly on the lips of modern critics. This "vanity of vanities" is supposed to be the latest thing in daring originality; as if there had never been a Preacher in Jerusalem, or such evergreen-sickness were a new thing under the sun! One difference indeed there is; Ecclesiastes, if like so many poets he had lost hope, had not lost also dignity and decency.

The words of Yeats do not apply only to the "troubles" of Ireland—

> We who seven years ago
> Talked of honour and of truth,
> Shriek with pleasure if we show
> The weasel's twist, the weasel's tooth.

And again—

> We are but critics, or but half create,
> Timid, entangled, empty, and abashed.

And because one extreme breeds another, this feeble-ness finds its counterpart in speeches by politicians holding it up as the highest crown of human life to litter with senseless carcasses some No Man's Land; and in a Europe that twenty years ago seemed civilized, intellectual freedom is persecuted in State after State with a systematic brutality unequalled since the religious persecutions of the seventeenth century—though there is left to-day no Dante or Milton, no Wordsworth or Byron, to speak for liberty. They might not be heard if there were. Modern poets and their critics between them have cured of ever buying new poetry that wider public for whose grandfathers a new volume by Tennyson or Browning or Arnold was an event. We can guess to-day what it was like to live in the twilight of the Roman Empire, with barbarism flooding back across the Danube and the Rhine; while our poets caress their incomprehensible Muses in select seclusion, like the Emperor Honorius feeding his pet hens in the marshes of Ravenna, as Alaric marched on Rome.

"Consider, for instance," continues meanwhile the voice of the modern critic, "the consummate reserve of this:

> Unable in the supervening blankness
> To sift TO AGATHON from the chaff
> Until he found his sieve...
> Ultimately, his seismograph."

Alas, the reserve is so "consummate" that it is like to have to do without being considered at all by a harassed world like ours. When Gérard de Nerval promenaded his living lobster on a dog-leash through the Palais-Royal, it was at least a novelty. To-day the highway of poetry is blocked with lobsters and laboriously eccentric gentlemen, begging the public to stop and overhear them

conversing in private code with the little black egos they
trail along our gutters. The public has ceased to stop.
And as if it were not enough that living poets should be
unintelligible, our critics father the same quality in
retrospect upon the dead. In a recent work with the
apocalyptic title, *Seven Types of Ambiguity*, it has been
revealed to an admiring public that the more ways
a poem can be misunderstood, the better it is. Take, for
example, Herbert's couplet—

> Ah, my dear God, though I be clean forgot,
> Let me not love thee, if I love thee not.

This, we are informed, means four different things—"If
I have stopped loving you, let me go"—"Let me not
love you in achievement, if I do not love you in desire"—
"Damn me if I don't stick to the parsonage"—and "Do
not make me hanker after you, if I would be better under
some other master elsewhere." For, our guide proceeds,
"it is a very reasonable deduction from the sexual
metaphor used by devotional poets that God should in
most cases be well scolded as a flirt". The significant
point about this sort of thing, which was praised to the
skies by stupefied reviewers, is not, I think, that so far
from meaning all four things at once the passage does
not mean any of them; nor yet that one of the explanations is not even English; nor yet that so much ingenuity
is squandered on a Philistine frivolity; but that the
attitude to poetry involved is so curiously vulgar. And
if there is one thing fatal to the writing or the appreciation
of poetry it is surely vulgarity. Men have written well
with, in the ordinary sense, bad enough morals; but not
with bad manners. When Sir Gawayne arrived in the hall

of the Green Knight, every one whispered overjoyed to his neighbour—"Now shall we see courteous conduct and blameless speech; now we shall learn noble manners." Can we feel they would have been equally rejoiced by the arrival of a contingent of modern gentlemen of letters, polished by six centuries of progress? It does not seem to me a matter of complete indifference that so much of the criticism that piques itself on being most "modern" should—to use the cant of the Communist—be "sabotaging" poetry.

For the qualities that the poets have valued seem to me what a world hag-ridden with theorists needs—above all that sense of the importance of the individual against the collective follies and brutalities of statecraft, which the poets have seldom forgotten, from the *Antigone* to Walt Whitman. We are stupidly afraid of this ferro-concrete colossus of modern science. The world has grown for the moment like some savage chief who has just had installed in his palace an electric-bell; it can think of nothing else, push nothing else, hear nothing else but this feverish tintinnabulation. But the basis of life remains unchanged—we are born, we love, we die—and nothing matters really but the states of mind or feeling, of contemplation or excitement, with which we fill our years; in which respect we are not noticeably better off than Socrates, nor yet noticeably better at producing more people like him. He had no electric-bells to listen to. Instead, he had a Demon. In some respects it worked better. And we have Poetry. The Gods of Hellas had a very able scientist among them, called Hephaestus. They did not tremble before him; they found him useful, but something of a joke; he was lame, for one thing, and sooty; yet they married him, some say, to Charis, who is Grace; or, as others tell, to Aphrodite, who is Loveliness. Might we not try to bring them together again?

There is indeed a danger that the progress of science may make us at once so powerful and so neurotic with the pace we live at, as to blow our wise selves out of existence altogether. But I believe that a new science may help redress the balance of the old—that science of psychology, of ourselves, which though still so raw has already done much to explain the morbid tangles of the mind and to make easier that directness and sanity which mark the poetry, above all, of Greece. For the poets have often seen clearly enough, since they looked at life as artists, not eaten up with the greed of possessing things, how absurdly we have over-complicated existence; until our minds are like those Victorian drawing-rooms we despise, every spare inch crowded with plush photographs and pincushions and puppies in porcelain. To clear one's life of dusty bric-à-brac—was not that the heart of the matter with Blake and Wordsworth and Arnold, with Morris and Meredith and Hardy? But a neurotic public prefers neurotic poetry. Our own generation, more overstuffed with impressions and more out of breath with chasing wild geese than any before, has made a god in its own likeness out of D. H. Lawrence; for that typical victim of its own diseases—of its industrialism, its barbarism, its brutal love of shouting on the housetops what sensible people have always known and never said—did yet feel instinctively what ailed his age, and had the gift of words to make men listen to the claims of the body, reasserted against the bloodless intellect. And in the same way is it not possible partly to sympathize with another figure equally fanatical, the leader who is trying to make Ireland turn her back on the stupid complexities of our civilization, in a self-sufficing simplicity alone with her Atlantic? In Germany the same exasperated craving for violent living and decisive action has found its figure-head in Hitler. The wages of Decadence are Fascism or Bolshevism. Where now are the intelligentsias of Russia and of Germany? Inevitably, the seedy intellectual calls up the noble savage, not always, alas, very noble; and the modern poet, trying to go one better than Shelley and be "an ineffectual devil" (mainly blue), is the very type that produces in the end, by scorn and loathing for itself, devils but too effectual.

In a word, the values of real life cannot remain without interest to poetry, if poetry is to be again of interest to the world, and not the autobiographical abracadabra of individuals mumbling at themselves in pocket-mirrors. And if its critics cared for such wider issues, they too might help. Yet genius is born without midwives. It can outlive their neglect. Some day we may dare to dream of a new Renaissance of understanding for Greek poetry; a new return to the sanity of Nature, less hysterical than Romanticism was; a new conviction, less narrow than in the age of Thomas Warton, that Nature, and sanity, and the wisdom of the Greek are but three guides in one.

All that I have urged, comes merely to this—that the criticism of poetry, whether professional or our own, though true interpretation be its first aim, unless it has also a keen sense of values remains but a blind sloth upon the Tree of Knowledge; that those values are not mere matters of subjective caprice—like the fineness of certain faces, they move us despite ourselves, because their worth has outlived in the real world the test of immemorial time; and that criticism cannot neglect these, to concentrate wholly on technical subtleties, without becoming a frivolous and shallow thing. "Good", in life itself as well as literature, is but the name we give to qualities that confer the vital power to survive. What matters in the end seems to me health, not holiness; sanity, not sin. And Beauty is not limited to what can be seen or heard or measured or poked. It is not in anatomical skill that the Laocoon is inferior to Olympia; not in technical cleverness that Dryden yields to Chaucer. Neither for poetry nor for criticism is cleverness enough. We are driven back to "Longinus"—to "the echo of a great soul". And indeed all our explanations of the eternal power of poetry come lamely to their journey's end. In the phrase of Vauvenargues—"Il faut avoir de l'âme pour avoir du goût"; in the words of his brother-soldier and fellow-critic, Sir Philip Sidney, denouncing those who can hear sweet tunes without "ravishing delight"—

Or if they do delight therein, are yet so closed with wit,
As with sententious lips to set a title vain on it;
Oh let them hear these sacred tunes, and learn in Wonder's
    schools
To be, in things past bounds of wit, fools if they be not fools!

EPILOGUE

In these pages it has been suggested that the fundamental quality of Romanticism is not mere anti-Classicism, nor mediaevalism, nor "aspiration", nor "wonder", nor any of the other things its various formulas suggest; but rather a liberation of the less conscious levels of the mind. Health, both in life and in literature, lies between excess of self-consciousness and excess of impulsiveness, between too much self-control and too little. The Romantic intoxication of the imagination suspends the over-rigid censorship exerted by our sense of what is fact and our sense of what is fitting. The first of these dominates the extreme Realist; both inhibit the extreme Classic; the Romantic escapes.

But it is not always into Paradise that he escapes. "Romanticism", said Goethe, "is disease." If Keats be disease, then let us have more of it. None the less Goethe has repeatedly proved right. Reality-principle and super-ego are not devices of the Devil: they are necessities of all civilized life. Again and again the Romantic who drinks too deep, who surrenders too much to the Unconscious, who becomes too completely a child once more, has fallen a victim to the neurotic maladies that beset the childish adult who cannot cope with life but falls between two ages. Then the "clouds of glory" have changed to the nightmares of ego-maniac perversion; to the love of sensation even in torture; to the pursuit of strange fruit even in the Garden of Proserpine, whose beauty is Death.

The advantage of the Freudian viewpoint is that it links together various characteristics of Romanticism, some healthy and some morbid, that hitherto seemed arbitrary and disconnected. Why, after all, should the same movement have led from Sir Galahad to *Salome*, from the Lady of the Lake to *La Charogne*, from chivalry to sadistic tortures, from idealism to ordure? Freud, like all pioneers, may often have got hold of the wrong end of the stick: it is hard to doubt that the sticks are there. About our infancy, it seems, lies Caliban as well as Ariel; after all, though it so horrified our grandparents, we accept the truth of that for the human race as a whole. And so the Romantic, I suggest, wandering in the Woods of Dream, has often wandered too far; and got lost like the neurotic who takes refuge from reality among the phantoms that haunt the mouldered lodges of his childish years. Those symptoms in individuals have become familiar; they are strangely like those of Romantic decadence.

But one may be the better for wine as well as the worse for it. The century since the Romantic Revival produced work of creative worth in greater abundance than any before it. Its criticism, too, became far more sensitive; but whereas eighteenth-century critics wrote often admirable sense or, if not, at least lucid nonsense, Romantic critics like Coleridge and Hugo and Carlyle and Ruskin and Swinburne, with all their brilliance, have tended to lapse into a transcendental nonsense far more tiresome to the reader. These star-gazers fall so easily into wells; and it is seldom Truth that they find at the bottom.

To-day, in the literature of the Many, Romanticism still reigns supreme; even in the literature of the Few its baser and more drunken offshoots seem to me far from extinct, though it is now a critical fashion to pose as

"Classical" and scorn Romanticism, as if it were not just as possible to have too little of it as too much. "The first important thing about contemporary literature", writes a modern critic, "is that it is contemporary." Unfortunately, it is often the last also. Pater thought, not very convincingly, that all art aspired to the condition of music; now it is to aspire to the condition of journalism. So we progress.

This may seem merely a matter of taste. On such, I have urged, it is vain for critics to debate; the only *general* judgements criticism can even attempt, I think, consist in saying, not "This is good" (good for what?), or "This is beautiful" (beautiful for whom?), but simply "This is true:[1] that is not", or "This looks sane; and this, diseased". It would be a great pity to banish writers like Baudelaire, as Plato would unhesitatingly have done. It is a great loss not to have read them. But it does not seem to me intelligent to ignore that such writers *are* diseased (as a great deal of genius is not); to live too much on, and with, them; or to forget that there remain certain advantages in being sane rather than morbid, sound rather than sick. And my complaint against much modern criticism is that it does forget these things; that it cares nothing if a writer is squalid, or brutal, or grovelling, or imbecile, provided he is "interesting" and leaves a new taste, however brassy, in the mouth. Our age is full of budding Baudelaires dyeing their heads green; when there is little enough need, with most of them, for that.

But even in theoretical criticism, though one may try to find a few general truths, ultimately one is still speaking

[1] I am aware that this word has many meanings; that does not mean it has none; merely that one must not muddle them.

of and for oneself, one's own values, one's own view of life. Looking back it seems to me that my own limited experience, through the twenty-two years since I went from Cambridge to the War, has only hardened these convictions by the test of time. In that No Man's Land, where one sat waiting for annihilation in a shell-hole, with the shells and speeches of both sides shrieking overhead, it was not mystics, religious or literary, that could bring support, but poets like Homer and Morris and Housman. I doubt if there is much modern literature that would stand that test, even for those who cheer it loudest in their armchairs. It is not the only test; but it is a severe one. And if the fatuity of modern Europe lets loose a new deluge, it will still be above all to the romantic Classicism of Greece, the romantic Realism of Iceland and of Hardy, the gaily realistic Classicism of eighteenth-century France that I shall look for consolation. They may fail; but I know none nearer to the truth of things.

LiT HisT